Nichole Nordeman is a wordsmith. I've always loved the writing of anyone who could take the alphabet and turn it into a little army of twenty-six soldiers, send them forth to march across a page, and occupy the territory with beauty, depth, poetry, humor, and truth. This is the talent of Nichole. We've heard it in conversations and listened to it in her music, but now for the first time, we have the privilege of reading her words in a book. It is my sincere delight to recommend *Love Story* to you. Don't miss it! With skill and incomparable giftedness, she teaches us biblical stories through the lens of her own humanity and touches us where we are, while lifting us to new heights.

luci swindoll
*author/speaker*

Turns out one of the best living lyricists is also a great author with some super-fresh insights and angles on the greatest story ever told. It's like Nichole actually had lunch with each of the characters before she wrote the chapters.

randy frazee
*author of* the heart of the story

We had the same experience reading this book that our whole family has had listening to the amazing lyrics Nichole wrote for *The Story* CD. Her willingness to use her incredible gift in such a brave and honest way makes the real people of the Story and the God of all our stories profoundly more real.

mary beth and steven curtis chapman
new york times *best-selling author; grammy and dove award-winning recording artist; founders of show hope, a movement for orphans*

I have always been spellbound by the songwriting of Nichole Nordeman. But here, amid the pages of her first book, it's confirmed to me that she really is one of the greatest writers of our time. Through her brilliant and creative storytelling, timeless Bible characters come to life in such a way, it's as if I'm walking in their shoes. And more than that, it's like they've walked in mine, because I find a little piece of me in every one. Thank you, Nichole. This book is a true treasure, as are you.

## natalie grant
*dove award winner; grammy-nominated singer/songwriter*

*Love Story* is nothing short of the greatest story ever told, now brilliantly retold in modernity by a master communicator. Nichole instantly and effortlessly manages to transcend the surface familiarity with the characters and stories of the Bible, bringing us into a stunningly beautiful, uncommonly insightful, wickedly humorous, equally tragic and triumphant, fresh encounter with Scripture. Woven together with her riveting and honest personal narratives, you will find yourself face-to-face with people of faith you only thought you knew. Perhaps the most remarkable thing is that, through the honest and empathetic lens of her own soul and trademark emotional intuition, Nichole makes us feel deeply again about the most important piece of literature in history.

## bernie herms
*dove award-winning, grammy-nominated producer/songwriter; producer and cowriter of* music inspired by the story

This book is not just a good read, it's a long walk with a friend. Nichole lets us put a glass up against the wall and hear what she and God have been talking about . . . and they've been talking a lot. She doesn't just give us information about God, but talks about His intention for us, lived out in what used to be just Bible stories to me. Nichole's writing style will have you seeing things differently. She'll make you wonder whether Jesus sometimes looked up at the clouds and thought they looked a little bit like us. That's because Nichole thinks we'll see most often what we love the most, and it's clear that Nichole sees God a lot.

## bob goff
*author of* love does; *founder and mischief maker of restore international; consul of republic of uganda*

# love
# story

*The Hand That Holds Us*
*from the Garden to the Gates*

# Nichole Nordeman

Cowriter of the Best-selling WOW! Album *The Story*

For Dan Wray.

You were the best teacher I ever had.

One day when I was fifteen, you told me I was a writer. But you said it like I was a bona fide grown-up with real live potential and not a teenage trainwreck with a bad perm. While it would take me years to believe it, when I finally faced this blinking cursor, yours was the voice I heard. Thank you.

# contents

foreword by al andrews     viii

introduction • *clutching clovers*     xi

creation • *the beginning of the end*     1

adam and eve • *how to kill a bird*     8

abraham and sarah • *what to expect when
you're not expecting*     23

joseph • *how to pray for a terrorist*     38

moses • *how to get unnoticed*     53

joshua • *circles in the sand*     68

ruth and naomi • *bridge and troubled water*     85

david • *why we watch the bleachers*     101

daniel • *getting lost, staying found*     114

esther • *gravy trains*     130

job • *when to make soup*     144

mary • *things to write in wet cement*     162

jesus • *glitter cows*     177

the thief • *steve and jesus*     192

mary magdalene • *gemology*     207

the disciples • *how to set a table*     223

paul • *when to cut class*     238

the second coming • *the end of the beginning*     255

*notes*     264

*acknowledgments*     265

# foreword

I spend a good portion of my days listening to the stories of others. As counselors, that's what we do. We hear people's narratives and try to guide them on a path toward healing.

Often when someone recalls a story from their past, I'm struck by their indifference to it. Overly familiar with the scene, they tell it as a newspaper reporter would write a story about something as interesting as the opening of an addition to the police station. It has become black-and-white and devoid of emotion or interest. Neither they nor I feel very engaged by it.

When this happens, I ask them to go back and sit with their story with fresh eyes, to reenter the scene as both an observer and a participant. Write it out, I request of them, remembering details, colors, smells, and emotions.

More often than not, they return with a new story. A once-lifeless description having been replaced by a living story with a heartbeat—joy and pain now in sharp color. They are engaged with it. They feel it. And they have become a part of it again. And then we can go to work.

When it comes to the familiar stories and characters of the Bible, I am often like that client with the familiar story. You say the name of a character and I can tell you the story. I know them well. Adam and Eve: Fig leaves. Snake. Got it!

Abraham and Sarah: Surprised old people have a baby. Father of many nations. Got it! Joseph: Coat of many colors. Tossed down a well. Check! And so on.

You may be like me in this regard—so familiar with the story that it has turned from its original and colorful truth. It lacks luster and impact.

Enter Nichole Nordeman and this lovely new book you now hold in your hand.

From the beginning, Nichole welcomes us as a delightful tour guide, takes our hands, and embarks with us on a journey. With her conversational tone and her wonderful humor, she invites us to visit the overly familiar Bible characters and return to sit with them again. Once there, she helps us to open the door to new treasures.

It is as if she has stationed herself at a new vantage point, and with her fresh sight uncovers truths that were aching to be revealed. In the most winsome of ways, she invites us into her inner thoughts, showing herself to be both vulnerable and real. Nichole is a hospitable writer, welcoming us into a story that she has made her home.

Until now, I've known Nichole Nordeman to be a singer and a lyricist. In the community of musicians, I have heard her described as the songwriter's songwriter. Her ability to transform the familiar into the holy with images and metaphors is uncanny and unparalleled. In her lyrics, she displays an intricate fusion of sorrow and hope. And now she has done all of this in a book, hopefully the first of many.

As you read *Love Story*, get ready for a rare and wonderful gift. Prepare to meet your inner three-year-old again—alive with wonder and teetering on the fence between laughter and tears, falling often on either side.

I am honored to call Nichole my friend. Though we have not known each other long, she has already become a trusted comrade. I want to take the rest of my life's sojourn with those who see what is real, grieve what is lost, laugh at themselves, and move ahead with hope. She is such a traveler.

The poet Mary Oliver once said this about her own craft: "Poetry is a life-cherishing force. For poems are not words, after all, but fires for the cold, ropes let down to the lost, something as necessary as bread in the pockets of the hungry. Yes indeed."

Mary Oliver could easily have been describing *Love Story*. Though it is prose, it is poetry as well, for you will find within its pages a fire to warm you, a rope to pull you up, and bread for your journey.

al andrews

# clutching clovers

I MOVED LAST YEAR.

Away from the big city to a slightly smaller city. But the change felt seismic.

My children, from infancy, have been nudged around in their overpriced strollers past endless hipster hangouts in our former urban downtown Dallas neighborhood. They blew kisses at coffee baristas. They hailed cabs with their pacifiers. They gobbled crunchy tempura shrimp rolls in their high-chairs at outdoor bistros.

For quite a while I thought this was fabulous because we so totally reeked of cool. But eventually I felt a nagging discontent about raising a family in the heart of a bustling downtown. I was wary of watching my son play with the single anthill on our zero-lot-line property. I was tired of dodging BMWs and boob jobs just to get a loaf of bread. I started obsessing about my own childhood. The bike rides. The cul de sacs. The tree forts. One day, my four-year-old encountered a cluster of trees at a city park, and exclaimed, "OH FOR HEHBENS SAKE, A FOREST!!!"

These moments sprouted small seeds that would eventually grow into our decision to move to Tulsa, Oklahoma, a few years later. Tulsa is very hilly and green, with trees aplenty. The first time I pulled into an ample parking space at the oversized mega-Target, I heard my minivan purr, "You had me at *Super*."

I made peace with the cliché of my life. We were suburban dwellers now and had delightful neighbors who smiled and waved at us. I had to yank the chain on my inner Labrador to keep from running across the lawn to lick their faces. It seems I had been a tad lonely for community. No longer reeking or even smelling faintly of cool, I now reeked of predictable, which was just wonderfully fine by me.

The downside, of course, was that I reeked of predictable, which was devastating.

To make myself feel better, I quickly sought out the part of town that had some personality and culture, in search of my people. I located the farmers' market, some local artisans and boutiques, an Irish pub, and a kind of freaky spiritual-ish used-book store, which is where I found myself happily browsing one Sunday afternoon. Despite my suspicion that most of the staff could offer me a tarot card reading on the spot, I ended up tucked away in the small Christian book section. Frankly, I was shocked they had one. I did not expect to find Beth Moore and Chuck Swindoll at the patchouli store.

One reason I have such a fondness for used books is that I am the nosiest person you'll ever meet. Not overtly nosy, of course. I'm not the annoying stranger at the Christmas party who interrogates you about every mundane part of your life or bores you with mine. I would never openly pry. But I'll say this, if I'm housesitting for you, don't leave your photo albums in plain view. And I will empty the contents of your purse onto the floor in a New York minute when you step away to use the restroom. I do feel bad about this sometimes. I just have an overactive curiosity about the innards of people's lives. (This does not, however, make me a gossip. I prefer to collect and keep my findings to myself. Which I guess makes me not only nosy but also a hoarder.)

A good used book, the margins all smudged in No. 2 pencil, dog-eared and with a respectable coffee or red-wine stain, is the ultimate treasure. For me, it means guilt-free eavesdropping, and it sets my imagination aflame. Who held this book? Why did they underline this passage? Why on earth *didn't* they underline that one? What inspired beauty and revelation? What bored them into a drooling stupor? A used book always connects me to the mystery of someone else's experience. And let me tell you, I can make up some epic stories about people I've never met who used to own a book I just bought.

To my surprise, wedged in between a few tight, tall shelves, was an enormous stack of old Bibles barely balanced on a vintage coffee table. With apologies for irreverence, these were not your average Bibles. They were not, as I like to call them, *Chicken Soup for Your Small Group* Bibles (*The Adventure Bible for Boys! Women Over 50 Bible! Bible for the Closet Pentecostal!*). Not those kinds. These were old and yellowy. Tissue thin in places. Equal parts smoothed and tattered by years spent in a great-grandfather's lap in front of the evening hearth during the long, bitter New England winters (*blah blah blah . . . see?*).

One Bible in the stack instantly hijacked my attention. It was absolutely enormous. So thick and heavy, I suspected some added material had been snuck in, which seemed easily possible since it looked old enough to have made the pre-Constantine cut. It was heavily ornate, swimming in black calligraphy, and dipped in gold a few times for good measure. It was hands down the biggest, fanciest Bible I'd ever seen. And I've been to Europe.

*Here* was a Bible that needed a story.

And so it came to pass that the Bible had lived in a cathedral on a mossy green hillside. It was kept in secret and safety inside a white marble vault, removed only by the senior-most priest to be read on the most hallowed of occasions. Like the king's nephew's wedding. The king of Oklahoma, perhaps. Clearly this Bible had been cradled in the hands of the faithful for centuries. It had blessed soldiers before battle and soothed many a mother's grieving heart at her son's funeral. Stalwart men of God had handled it with white-gloved reverence. It was kept the way Scripture was intended to be kept . . . with deep and chronic care.

I do not exaggerate. It was that fancy.

I knew I wouldn't find pencil marks in the margins, but I opened it anyway. I wanted to trace my fingers over the gossamer pages, wondering if it might leave some special sacred residue on my skin. I suspected it might momentarily make my own faith seem small and Western and dot-com-ish.

Which it kind of did.

I started in the book of Psalms, lifting and turning each page like 14-karat Kleenex and began to feel indignant about what kind of loathsome no-good nephew of a king allows a Bible like this to land in a used bookstore in Tulsa.

Which is when I spotted the first one.

A perfectly pressed and preserved four-leaf clover, snuggled safely in between Psalm 50 and 51. I stared at it for the longest time. It was just so . . . *odd.* And lonely. I started frantically rewriting the storyline, slightly annoyed because senior-most priests don't pluck clovers. A gift for the nephew's Irish bride, I wondered?

The little clover was not so lonely after all. I spent some time there with the Bible in my lap and found close to *thirty* more perfect four-leaf clovers tucked neatly throughout the entire text. Anyone who's spent any time crouching cross-legged in a field with a child looking for these suckers knows how much patience it would take to find that many of them over a lifetime. I was forced to abandon the cathedral bit and became increasingly incensed that somebody had sold Grandpa McNeely's family Bible at the garage sale, caring nothing for his clover collection. A slap in the ruddy face of all Ireland. Appalling.

I probably sat on the floor for an hour, reading that Bible. Carefully touching but not removing the clovers. Wondering why a person with a sophisticated enough faith to own such a spectacular and holy Book would care about preserving so many silly symbols of good luck. And then it dawned on me rather abruptly that this particular story was not about the cathedral. Or Grandpa McNeely.

It was about me.

This is, and has always been, the way I've read the Bible . . . with my fingers crossed, muttering, "pleaseletthisbetrue" under my breath.

With a rabbit's foot for a bookmark.

I *do* believe God's Word. I claim its promises. I have a healthy knowledge of its contents. But for as long as I can remember, there has always been this small and cynical whisper in my soul that suggests I am really just clutching at clovers. That over the course of history, mankind has so falsified and neutered God's original intent that we're only reading flecks and specks of lingering truth. It's a bit like the old children's game of telephone with the soup cans. I trust the source, just not the cans.

Frankly, there is so much in Scripture that is quite literally unbelievable. For so long I have asked, prayed, and begged that I could possess the kind of faith that would just take the Bible at face value. I know and admire so many people who don't give it a second thought. If you grow up in the church or in Christian education (or are a Christian recording artist) this is sort of 101 material. Biblical inerrancy is a deal breaker for most evangelicals. And yet, years later, I'm still asking God to free my belief from the bonds of my intellect.

Some time ago, my manager of fifteen years invited me to participate in cowriting songs for a project called *Music Inspired by The Story*. The idea was to write songs about the most familiar and beloved Bible characters. But first, I needed to read my Bible through a new lens. Not for the big takeaway lesson or historical context or some tidy pastoral acronym but instead through the lens of humanity. Through the first-person lens of the actual people whose lives are spilled out on its pages. Not to hear more *about* them but to hear *from* them.

This meant I was to really listen and consider what God whispered to every disbelieving and disillusioned straggler who wagged a finger at the absurdity of God's call on their lives. I was invited to scratch below the sheen of the "hero of our faith" tattoo that labeled these men and women who had paraded around in my head my whole life. And then, once I had understood them to be really human, to write some songs about what they might have said. Or cried. Or sung. To give them a modern voice that might ring a small bell of recognition of what our Author sees in us.

God and I had a really good belly laugh over this opportunity. I mean, we were like doubled over, wiping away tears at the whole idea. Backs were slapped. He knew, of course, how totally unqualified I would be to assert any biblical insight with my own handicap blinding me, and I wholeheartedly agreed.

He also knew, once I had a good laugh, that I would readily accept the invitation, much like a moth, with little choice, is drawn to the flame. Actually, he seemed to think it was a good idea.

I signed on for the project right around the time I held the clover Bible and spent the afternoon spinning fake stories about its imagined owner. Now I would wait and see what stories he would reveal about the real people inside. And what true stories he wanted to write on my own pages.

I knew very little about the journey ahead. I wondered if it might finally put periods where question marks had taken up residence for so long. But I sort of doubted that.

Me. Doubting. Big shocker.

The one small certainty I had was that I had every freedom to excavate my questions and that I would be well loved in the process. And as it turns out, I was not alone in that certainty. Because in every story, and on every page, from the garden to the gates, I encountered God's people tucking his love into their satchels, sewing it into their robes, clutching it in fear, clawing at in anger, carving it into caves, collapsing into it, re-joicing, repenting, revising and rewriting their stories because they were . . . we are . . . so perfectly loved.

The Bible is the ultimate used Book that's falling apart in perfect condition, much like its cast of characters.

Love stories, all of them.

Now, having spent a good deal of time eavesdropping, I'd like to share some things I scrawled in the margins.

Maybe it pays to be nosy.

*creation*
# the beginning of the end

IN THE BEGINNING, God created the heavens and the earth.

Somethingness from nothingness.

Fullness from emptiness.

Presence from vacancy.

The great week of wonder had begun.

With Genesis chapter 1 open in my lap, I watch him cut the ribbon. I hear the shovel break ground at the new construction site, and I snap a mental picture of God in a hard hat, all smiles. He is about to blow our minds.

And he does, says Pastor Ed one Sunday, but pay closer attention to *how*. Creativity follows a distinct pattern that God put in place. Even in his hands, creation does not make the journey from wasteland to wonder in a blink. There are some subtle middle moments to consider.

First, he simply speaks the heavens and earth into existence. He does not call them good but instead, one breath later, describes the miracle of this new creation as formless, void, and empty,[1] the Spirit still hovering over the deep. That seems like an odd declaration after such an accomplishment. Let there be earth! (*Huh. Kinda void-ish.*)

Creation is on a sure path to goodness, but now, even in the hands of the Creator, it is in process first. Still in chaos.

Next God clears his throat to address the darkness, whispering the name of its new counterpart . . .

Let there be *light*.

Spectacular.

Terrifying.

Light slashing madly down the middle of the heavy dark drapes, scattering shards of thin black to the farthest corners of the universe. If any angels were brave enough to stay for the show, I suspect they had to turn away for parts of it, drawing in sharp breaths, dwelling in wide, worried silence. Heads shaking, wings tucked.

Light from darkness the first day. Astonishing. And still, no mention of "good." The heavens are seething with potential, but on this day, we are left again to confront that vague space that dangles between vision and completion.

It's how he set up the design process for every artist that would follow. The work of all creativity must first be subjected to agony and toil. It must be lingered over. It must languish. Picked up, turned around, set down. It must find order and stability. Every brushstroke and lyric and clay pot and arabesque and sonnet. Any moment, no matter how small, that seeks to reflect the Creator must travel this lonely predawn road. The Spirit must hover and hover over our deep darkness. That is, if it is to be called good.

Which perhaps is why so much "art" just isn't. There is no evidentiary trace of his likeness.

I consider these first few moments of creation: Heavens. Earth. Light. Darkness. It is not good yet. But it is there; it is ready. And something in me wants to stand up in the middle of the passage and yell, "STOP! STOP RIGHT THERE. Please God, don't feel obligated to see this thing through. Because in a few short days you will be sculpting the antelope's antlers and telling us how good it is. But we know how this week ends. And it's not good at all. So please, in your compassion, spare us this needless spiral into hopelessness."

But he doesn't stop. He is in love with potential. As he always has been.

I can't shake off my questions in the creation story. If God is God and knows all things past, present, and future . . . if he already knew about the runaway train on the tracks ahead, why did he create at all? The most cynical part of me wants to call it the "Why bother?" story.

Why bother with every luminous shade of orange on the flimsy wing of a monarch if he knows how the story will end?

Did he know when he separated the sky from the water that we would find endless and creative ways to destroy both? Did he know then that we would dump jet fuel mid-flight? That we would send spaceships into his carefully ordered atmosphere and clutter it with debris? When he spoke the ozone layer into existence for our protection, did he know about hairspray in the eighties?

And when, with outstretched hands, he spoke the oceans and seas into place, did he know we would spill oil everywhere? That we would dump our toxic waste into the mouths of creatures great and small who call the water home?

If he knew, why fret over the number of starfish arms? (*Six? No, five is best.*)

Why bother?

When God called the dry ground "land," could he have known what we would do with it? The concrete we would pour? The mines we would gouge in our greedy hunt for riches until entire mountain ranges were stripped bare? The forests lost? The soil depleted? The fires set?

Did he know, that first week, how we would divide ourselves eventually? Claiming certain sections of dirt for our own tribes? Erecting borders? Inventing *us* and *them*? Like children scattered beneath a broken piñata, scrambling and shoving what we can into our pockets before running for the corners to count the loot?

This is our legacy with land. Did he know?

Then came the cucumbers and olives, wheat fields and peach trees. The day he created, with color and flavor, every good and nourishing thing, did he see on that day the jutting ribs of starvation? The bulging, gluttonous bellies hung heavy over elastic pants? Did he see us filling our bodies with matter but not with the nutrients he'd carefully engineered? Surely, had he known about pork rinds he never would have let us feed ourselves but would have built solar panels across our backs for energy instead.

The day he made the swift deer and gentle elephant, did he see poaching?

When he patched together the smooth scales of the alligator, did he see handbags?

Did he know about the circus?

Did he know his beautiful kingdom of creatures would become our collective lab rat?

I mean, really, why bother?

Could he have ever imagined, on the day he blew life into the nostrils of marvelous man, the crown of his creation, that we would so utterly destroy one another?

That our carefully painted shades of skin would barbarically entitle us to own each other? That a bloodline would spark genocide? That we would kill, maim, and extinguish and, to make matters more devastating, that we would often do it in his name?

"You can safely assume that you've created God in your own image when it turns out that God hates all the same people you do," a friend tells the incomparable Anne Lamott.[2]

Did God stand in the garden, seconds away from breathing life into Adam, and try to push aside the inevitable thoughts of rape, suicide, sex slavery, abortion?

If he knew the ending, then why set even the beautiful beginnings of it in motion?

I believe he did know. He couldn't be God otherwise.

I don't think he began and then completed his whole work in a week and then, one rascally serpent and an apple later, had to come up with a redemptive ending on the fly. I don't think he was standing there in front of trembling Adam and Eve with his hand on his hip thinking, *Well, howdaya like that? Figures.*

Of course he knew we would toss a grenade into all that beauty.

As he swept across the surface of our new planet, paying close attention to the fox's tail and the cricket's legs and the buds on a rosebush, it was then that he seemed pleased with his work. This is when it was good. Not in the chaotic hovering nameless space but only once his hands had created life. Because God *is* life. And he caught a glimpse of his own reflection. And it was very, very good.

I wonder if, instead of feeling the weight of our inevitable and deplorable stewardship, he found glimpses of hope and purpose when he thought of us that first week.

He knew Adam would need to cover himself with leaves.

He knew Abraham would need stars to count and Joseph would need grain to share.

He knew Moses would need a rock to strike and a shepherd boy named David would need a few smaller stones. Ruth would need a field to harvest. We'd need lots of trees. To build an ark for animals. And an ark of the covenant. To build a manger. And a cross. And we would need some clouds. A pillar to follow in the desert wilderness.

Many more to scroll back for his return.

In all of these moments, the Creator held us like newborns and saw glimpses of himself. And though it is our capacity for utter darkness and destruction that leaves me wondering why he bothered, it is our capacity to reflect the perfection of his light and love that reveal why he did. Of course he bothered.

It was good then because he was good.

And it will be good always because love knows no other way to be.

*adam and eve*
# how to kill a bird

I AM NOT a person who has debilitating phobias. You hear about people who encounter spiders or planes or large crowds of people and immediately start doing the backstroke through their own cold sweat. Not me. I might be a teeny bit claustrophobic but usually only around people who have bad breath and are close talkers. So I wouldn't call my one tiny little fear an actual phobia, but I will admit that I am not a bird lover. At all.

When I was little, I was not allowed to use the word *hate*. So ingrained was this rule that I still struggle to say it, even when I really mean it. My frustrated angry teenage moments felt totally neutered by my limited vocabulary. Slamming a door in your mother's face and screaming, "I seeeeriously detest your guts!" was less than cathartic. *Hate* packs a punch. So I'll stop short of saying I hate birds. I don't hate them. I just seeeeriously detest their little guts.

Birds are the last creatures I want to get near, much less aid in any way. I don't care if you are holding a cardboard Will Work for Seed sign on the exit ramp. I don't care if you need someone to take you to rehab or need lunch money or a letter of recommendation for college admission. If you are a bird, don't bother asking me for anything because I pretty much *h*-word you.

And this is coming from a bona fide animal lover. Truly. I've picked up more stray pets and made more LOST posters than you can imagine, but I would offer shelter to a wild, seething boar before some helpless, gawky pigeon.

In reflecting on this disdain I've felt through the years, I've concluded that it's not really a bird thing. It's a quick-movement thing. It's a flutteryness issue. If you can move faster than I can, if you can swoop or peck or dip and dive or flap flap flap, we can't be friends. The truth is, I'm just terrified of you. I guess the same is true for anything that darts or scurries. Squirrels, roaches, mice. I might have a little scurriphobia. Attention, small creatures of earth: slow down already!

I can trace the genesis of my flappy fear issues back to a time when I was broke and in real need of any extra work that was legal, so I accepted a bird-sitting gig for a friend of a friend who would be out of town for a few days. She just needed someone to house-sit Ivan the cockatoo. I assumed he needed a refill of his food and water dish and not much else.

The first day, I let myself in with the spare key, nodded to Ivan, secure in his cage, and plopped down on the couch to read no fewer than ten pages of instructions, a lot of them in CAPS. For instance . . .

1. Ivan can easily sense fear. Your fear makes him fearful, which makes him aggressive. DO NOT SHOW FEAR.

2. When you are in the house, please let him out of the cage so he can fly around and exercise. You will know if he senses your fear if he starts to swoop down from the curtain rod toward your head. SILLY BIRD!

3. If you sense that he is going to be aggressive, just whistle a song. ANY SONG. And he will perch on your shoulder and settle down. Attached is a list of favorite songs. . . .

4. DO NOT USE AEROSOL HAIRSPRAY when you are in the bathroom because he will probably be perched on your shoulder while you are fixing your hair, and it could KILL him.

The instruction manual went on like this for pages. Nay, days.

I will spare you the horrifying play by play. Let's just say Hitchcock would have felt like a poser in the scenes that followed. And let's also say I drank alone for the first time. And that I never really learned how to whistle as a child. Fill in the rest as you see fit.

All of this bird baggage from my past made last week even stranger. My bedroom has this one absurdly high window shaped like a half moon that sits over the balcony doors. I'm sure it has a proper window name, but I just call it "the uncleanable." This window can seduce afternoon sunlight so beautifully that I fall in love with my bedroom around 3:00 p.m. every day because it looks like Rapunzel has been washing the walls with her golden hair.

So I'm folding laundry around this time, when I hear and see a red-breasted robin bonk into the uncleanable, which is the worst sound ever, even if you *h*-word birds. The robin startled me but then disappeared. I assumed he had learned his lesson and moved on.

Wishful thinking.

*Bang. Bang! Tap. Flutter. Tap. Clunk. Flutter.*

I started freaking out.

*Tap. Clunk.*

This seemed to continue for agonizing ages.

After every big *bonk,* the robin would fly off for a few minutes and regroup. I imagined a little bird trainer somewhere, giving him a quick shoulder massage and a towel smack on his rear. Get back in there, champ.

*Flutter. Tap. Clunk.*

I was beside myself.

Even for me and my bird ~~hatred~~ sensitivity, this was too painful. I couldn't understand the tenacity that sent him repeatedly trying to fly into a window that so clearly would never permit his entrance. Some switch of compassion flipped inside me. I started yelling and waving my arms like I was holding orange glow sticks on a tarmac. Go thaaaat way. Over theeere.

*Flutter. Smack.*

On it went.

I ran outside around the house, not caring who saw or heard. Yelling, trying to entice the robin with incentives that worked for my three-year-old. "Yoohooooo! I have Cheetos! Hey look, Robin, Santa!!!"

He would not be deterred. He was committed and convinced if he smacked into my window one more time, he would fly in freely. I was racked with guilt. *If he continues, he dies. If he continues and does not die, then I will have to find a large can of aerosol hairspray and get down to business.* Which made me wonder, why was I so panicked about saving a creature I didn't really want to save?

This went on every afternoon for days. I felt sick that I could not help this thing I loathed. Then my friend Jill, who is painfully adept at pointing out the obvious, said, "Dude. Same thing happened to me. Birds are really dumb. They just see their own reflection in the glass and try to fly toward it but get confused. Just hang something in front of the window so it stops seeing itself. Problemo solvo."

Oh.

But before I could locate a ninety-foot ladder to hang anything up in front of the uncleanable, the clunking and fluttering abruptly ceased, and I realized, with great relief, that my robin had finally stopped trying to rendezvous with its own reflection and had moved on. And there was, once again, peace in the land.

Until I walked outside a few days later and realized he had indeed moved on . . . to bird heaven. (Which I'm certain is nowhere near people heaven.) He looked so small and pitiful lying on his back on my balcony. While I was zipping up my hazmat suit preparing to dispose of him, I actually felt true sadness. Obviously there is a natural order to things and he would have died someday anyway, but it was *how* he died that made me so sad. He died of madness, I think. Fluttering and hovering in front of his reflection for days. Yearning to be with that other self. Never understanding the way reflective glass lies. And confuses. And distorts.

My run-in with the robin came as I was beginning to write songs for *The Story,* starting with a peek inside the humanity of Adam and Eve. Maybe because I was already in a fragile state due to the robin's demise, I felt tremendous sadness for them. And also a great deal of understanding, because I've always felt that original sin was not disobedience but misplaced desire.

What happened in the garden of Eden makes for such a weird tale. Fruit trees and talking snakes and shameful lies. It's so hard to really put myself there mentally because it almost feels like it was lifted out of Narnia. My imagination wanders. Did other animals talk too? When God walked with Adam and Eve in the cool of the day, did he really walk with them physically? Was he tall? And why, after God delivers his devastating verdict and punishment, does Adam only then name his wife? And why, especially, does he give her a name that means "life" in a moment that was essentially soul death? I'll spare you the countless other questions and save them for God when we meet.

I know it's easy to read the story and feel smug, as if we would have certainly chosen otherwise. My inner cynic demands, "Was complete utopia not quite enough for Eve? Was she not satisfied enough with her burden-free life, nestled in paradise, wanting for nothing, and lunching with God? How do you actually experience the grass-is-greener phenomenon in *Eden,* lady?!"

And Adam. Could he not have found the courage to challenge Eve's decision to eat the fruit? Did he not possess enough conviction or bravery to stand up to a naked lady and an apple? Not exactly Goliath, buddy. Way to man up.

In our sophisticated modern faith, we shake our heads at their choices. We blame our personal pain and the whole world's ills on that pivotal moment, the fall. When we don't know how to explain away broken hearts or hurricanes or cancer or war, we point to Adam and Eve and say, "Hey, thanks a lot, guys."

Of course, there's truth in tracing the path of darkness right back to a shady tree and a tragic choice, but I think Adam and Eve get a bad rap. Because I know this much: if we had managed to live in peace and harmony in the garden for thousands upon thousands of years, all of creation in a perpetual state of spotless obedience and blissful paradise until the twenty-first century, *I* would have been the one who wrecked it all to pieces.

It would have been me listening to the serpent's whispers, considering his claims, sniffing the fruit, rolling it around in my palm, walking away with a fake disinterest and then hurrying right back a few minutes later to pick it up again. It would have been my teeth sinking into its ripe flesh. It would

have been my sin that rippled right into the wave of hopelessness that all of humanity is forever bobbing around in, trying
to keep our heads above.

So I guess I never spent a lot of time pointing a finger at
them. It was gonna happen eventually.

Their sin was that they wanted to be more than they were
intended to be. They wanted to see and know more than they
were intended to see and know. What's so wrong with that? I
listen carefully to the serpent's claim, "God knows that when
you eat from it, your eyes will be opened, and you will be like
God, knowing good and evil."[1]

Actually, the serpent wasn't lying about all of it. They, of
course, would never be *like* God, but their eyes would indeed
be opened and they would know good and evil. That was the
hook. The snake insinuated that if eating the fruit would open
their eyes, it must mean their eyes were somehow currently
closed. They must have thought, *Is God keeping something
from us? Are we not the crown of his creation—and yet he
clearly hasn't trusted us with certain things. I think we should
know too! It's only fair.*

That snake coiled himself slowly and quietly around their
pride and then started squeezing.

Or, I wonder, could it be that they loved God so fiercely
and completely that they just wanted to be like him? Not in
the way that we use that phrase now but to be like him literally—like some perverse form of the ultimate flattery. *Maybe,*
they hoped, *if we know what God knows, it might deepen our*

*relationship with him and our understanding of life somehow. We'll be God! What could be better than that?*

Just about anything.

It's hard to be exactly who you were made to be and not want more. It's hard not to confuse bettering yourself with betraying yourself. It's hard not to keep smacking into the glass, certain you can be at one with your pretty reflection.

*Flutter. Clunk.*

That's how I know I would have chosen what Eve chose that fateful day. I'm always trying to open my eyes too wide. We are bombarded by so many messages about self-improvement. I'm not just talking about Oprah's age of enlightenment, which is an easy target. And actually, I've learned quite a bit from Ms. Winfrey. But the church is keeping pace as well. We are slathered in slogans: "Taking it to the next level" or "Write a better story for yourself" or "Come grow with us!" The idea itself is spot-on. Quit stagnating in your life or your faith. Get off your couch and live fully in God's dream for you.

Sign me up.

The danger, for me, is that I get so caught up in the "bigger, better, deeper, fuller, more" that I can become deaf to God's voice begging me to not be dazzled by the promise of what I could become but to find value and security in just being who I am and where I am. I wish Adam and Eve could have rested in that. I wish I could.

Awhile back, my mom visited. She was folding a few loads of my laundry, as moms will do, and said rather unceremoniously, "Sweetheart, I noticed that everything you own is gray."

I glanced at two large stacks of neatly folded shirts, pants, and hoodies, all in varying shades of dark and light gray. We laughed, a quiet river of understanding running between us.

It's no secret to anyone who really knows me that I've been very depressed for the past year. It's been a real doozy. I haven't battled depression in my life except briefly after the birth of my son, which I'm still convinced is because he projectile-vomited in my face after every meal for six months.

In fact, I used to be one of those dreadful types who encountered struggling souls wrestling with depression and would sort of spit random encouraging Bible verses at them, wondering why they couldn't just snap out of it. You know, dig deep and find some gratitude. Take a brisk walk or something.

But if you've ever really been seriously depressed, you know that the physical weight you carry around is very real. You can't take a brisk walk because you can't tie your shoes. There have been days in the recent past when getting out of bed to feed my kids breakfast and then later on, fill the car with gas and *still* after *all that* remember to brush my teeth, felt like scaling Mount Olympus. It's been a really dark time. Every day underwater, slow and blurry.

I went to Chicago to celebrate my fortieth birthday (gee, turning forty helped) with my best friend, Amy, who lives there. She pretty much took one look at me and my weight gain, slogging around in my frumpy gray jacket and black scarf, and insisted I get some antidepressants. Not forever, she reassured me; just until the cloud lifts and I could face what needs facing. We talked at great length. She said her birthday gift to me was that she was going to stalk me until I called my doctor, which stunk because, since we had recently moved to a new city, I hadn't even found a doctor yet, so this meant telling my sob story to a total stranger. (Sorry if all this makes you uncomfortable. I know people normally write about this stuff after it's all better.)

I reluctantly agreed. I knew she was right. Then she added, "Dang, I wish I could come with you."

"I know. Thank you."

"Well, to support you, of course, but really, I'd like to be there to out you."

"Out me?"

"I just know you, Nichole, and you will totally downplay how depressed you are because you'll be far more focused on creating a great first impression and hoping you're his new favorite patient. You will try to dazzle and befriend him. You have to be honest. You *need* to wear gray to this appointment. You have plenty."

*Sigh.*

It's a bittersweet thing to be really known by someone. All the rocks you normally hide under have already been over-turned. She was right. The thought of telling the truth about myself, even to a doctor who's heard far worse, completely paralyzed me. I am so conditioned to present a certain self.

Confident. Engaging. Friendly. Funny. Everything I see when I'm frantically flapping my wings in front of that glass but can never really, fully be.

Weepy and unraveling is not on that list.

I did as I promised I would. I went home, got a recommendation for a doctor from a friend, called, and made the dreaded appointment. I was on hold for like eight minutes and almost hung up eight times. Finally, the receptionist picked up and started looking at the calendar for the next available appointment, which—lo and behold—was the very next day because of a cancellation. I almost threw up. This gave me zero time to rehearse my lines. To practice in front of the mirror. To carefully research all of the medication options so my doctor could marvel at his new patient's wealth of knowledge and information.

I prayed so hard that night. Big, rolling tears pooled symmetrically on either side of my pillow as I lay staring at the dark ceiling. Praying that maybe this doctor's appointment might be a lily pad. Not strong enough to sustain me forever but buoyant enough to keep me from going under. I prayed to see myself as God sees me, not as my hazy, messed-up reflection. To stop slamming into the uncleanable.

True to form, I woke early and started working on the first impression. I tried to remember how to wear makeup and how to fix my hair in something other than a greasy ponytail. I started practicing how to present my brokenness without sounding broken. Amy texted me while I was driving to the appointment. *Praying for you. You feel ready?* I glanced down. I was wearing a bright red blouse and a cool bracelet. And heels. Everything on the inside of me was disappearing into quicksand, and everything on the outside said, "Hors d'oeuvres and cocktails at eight! Come, won't you?"

*Flutter. Flutter. Thud.*

It didn't matter.

I took one look at the kindness behind the doctor's eyes and lost any lower lip control.

He handed me Kleenex and spoke with me for almost an hour with great compassion, great hope, and great respect. I never even got to tap dance.

I met a girl recently who makes really cool custom jewelry. I asked her to make me a necklace with a fig-leaf charm. When I feel it press against my neck or catch a glimpse of it in a mirror, I remember that falling doesn't have to mean hiding. I remember Adam and Eve and how they really fell—not because they succumbed to some evil lurking in their hearts or because they felt so compelled to defy God's careful instructions, but perhaps because they fell in love with the poisonous suggestion that they could be who they were never created to be. And in doing so, fell out of true relationship with the only One who could have told them the truth, had they asked.

I wear that fig-leaf necklace because I want to remember that every minute of every day I am one bite away from falling down just like that. Just like the robin. Falling in love with the image in the glass. Falling away from what's real. Falling down dead with exhaustion.

This is my prayer right now:

Creator and Lover of all of us, help me see you reflected in me, and not just more of me reflected in me. And let that be more than enough sweet fruit for today.

*Then the man and his wife heard the sound*
*of the LORD God as he was walking in the garden*
*in the cool of the day, and they hid from the LORD God*
*among the trees of the garden. (Genesis 3:8)*

# good
## *adam and eve*
### Lyrics from *Music Inspired by The Story*

If I could, I'd rewrite history.

I'd choose differently,

If I could, I would.

I'd leave out the part where I broke your heart in the
garden's shade,

Fix the mess I made.

If I could, I would.

If I could, close my eyes and then dance around again.

If I could, I would be who you adored.

Why did I need more,

When beauty was not trained to hide behind my
shame?

If I could, I would.

Can you hear us cry?
Wishing we could turn back time,
To feel your breath when branches move,
Take one more sunset walk with you.
Must each tomorrow hold such brokenness untold?
Can't imagine how you could
See all of me and say it's good.

If I could, hold one memory,
It would surely be how you walked with us.
I'd go back in time,
Untell my first lie,
And let Love's injury heal in spite of me.

It is good.
It is good.
You still love us more than we believed you could.
Could there be something more?
Will it ever be the way it was before?

*abraham and sarah*

# what to expect when
# you're not expecting

I ALMOST NEVER travel anymore. I've become such an embarrassing amateur at it now. I'm the person you avoid getting stuck behind in the airport security line because I thought I remembered the liquids rule being thirty ounces, not three. I'm the gal trying to empty eight dollars' worth of dimes from my pockets before I take my sweet time unlacing my thigh-high pirate boots. I used to be able to pull off that whole security-drill thing blindfolded. Now I'm the mouthy genius that can evacuate a terminal in five seconds: "Riiiiight, like I'm hiding a PIPE BOMB in my lip gloss, people . . ."

Despite some recent and humiliating patdowns, I actually made it through security without incident this past weekend to spend a few days on the West Coast. It's always a good thing when my work takes me to Southern California. I have quite a lot of family scattered out there, and I usually jump at any chance to tack on a little extra pleasure time to whatever business I might have. Headed to LA for a quick meeting,

I decided to fly in a day early to spend some time with my grandma, who turns ninety-two in a few months.

Each time I visit, I mentally prepare myself to see her looking fragile and frail, staring off into a starry space where old memories collide with real time in a confusing cloud. I expect to feel her thin shoulders disintegrate just a little when I hug her, and I just assume she'll smell like Jell-O or Ensure. I expect to nod politely for hours at retold stories and answer the same questions about myself twelve times. These things are a natural part of the aging process, I tell myself as I brace for all the new ways that time has rendered her unrecognizable to me.

Then she opens her door, and I realize I've been mentally preparing to visit someone else's grandma. She's doing just fine.

On her best dishes, over Subway sandwiches, I learn in the first ten minutes that she is done with Jimmy Fallon. I mean, she's *had* it with that clown. Evidently there was a segment on his show recently making fun of a ninety-something-year-old man who married an eighty-something-year-old woman, and Jimmy just could not get enough mileage out of mocking the absurdity of their sex life.

"If you have to make fun of old people having marital relations, you have no business being a comedian," she announced. "We're not a sideshow at the circus. We're human beings. I don't have to listen to his stupid dirty sex talk anymore."

I laughed out loud. But not in the condescending way our culture usually winks at older generations for being irrelevant but really cute. I laughed with joy because I love that she is still so totally engaged in life and in the world around her. And because she was totally right. Making fun of old-people sex is some pretty low-hanging fruit, Jimmy.

She is fully alive. Sharp as a tack. Hilarious. And brimming with passionate commentary on every political, religious, or social ailment in modern memory, should any unfortunate soul wander by her house and ask her to elaborate.

We watched her great-grandson's middle-school talent show on YouTube. We ate German chocolate cake. I blew seven inches of dust off her turntable, and we played her old Ray Charles records plus a few Burl Ives and the soundtrack from *The Sound of Music.* I made her tell me the story again about how George Beverly Shea ended up in their apartment in Australia, playing my grandpa's organ after a Billy Graham crusade. We went through her books too, the ones on the very top shelf I hadn't seen before. A copy of *Pilgrim's Progress* from 1905. A collection of Longfellow poetry. An edition of Aesop's fables so timeworn I was afraid to turn the gauzy pages.

I realized pretty quickly that this was not just another afternoon stroll down memory lane with her but that she was really trying to give me these things that were special to her, not knowing when I'd visit next. She'd hand me a treasure and say nonchalantly, "You know, that's probably worth some money now . . . ," knowing full well I would clutch my heart and say, "Not in a million years would I sell that, Grandma," and mean it.

And she would shrug her shoulders indifferently but smile deep on the inside.

These are unchartered emotional waters for us. We both understand that one day death will come, as death will do rather reliably. Quickly for some. For others it waits ninety or so years. But it's really hard to sit comfortably and hold someone's hand with the mutual awareness that your time left together is probably short. These are the moments when we often fail ourselves and each other with our words and silences. We avert our eyes and start whistling something snappy in a moment that begs for transparency and acceptance.

Many times during the day Grandma spoke casually about her inevitable passing, so much that it bordered on fixation. Each time my inner adolescent wanted to blurt out, "Oh, yooou! Don't be silly! You're gonna outlive us all, Miss Thang!"

If I had, we'd probably both manage a small chuckle, but inside I would know what an awful choice I'd made. A wonderfully easy and awful choice. A long and well-lived life deserves, at the very least, our refusal to tiptoe around the final lap. Imagine running a marathon for ninety-plus years only to find nobody openly cheering at the finish line because sitting in the bleachers is too hard for *them*.

The only other time I remember being in that same clumsy heart space was with my father-in-law the week before he lost his battle with lung cancer. He sat across from me on the couch with an awkward half smile and asked if I would sing at his memorial service. He was not an outwardly emotional man, and I knew this conversation was costing him a lot. I clenched my jaws for the longest time to suppress the temptation to sidestep and mutter something optimistic about prayer and miracles. When I was confident my words would not betray me, I forced myself to look up through a curtain of tears until I found his eyes.

Of course.

Of course, I will.

These beautiful moments and painful promises nudge me toward the story of Abraham and Sarah. We have so much to learn from the gray gathered at their brows. Their lives are magnificent teachers, often in unexpected ways. We meet them for the first time in Genesis 12, when God tells them to leave family and country and set out for a new land he's promised. Abraham is seventy-five when this adventure begins. Read that again if you're feeling irrelevant and past your perky prime. *He was seventy-five.*

God tells him to uproot everything. Don't ask questions. Start packing. I'll handle the details. Just hit the road, Jack.

Okay, God.

Right off the bat, Abraham's teaching us about blind faith. Then, after he follows God out of his homeland, we get a front-row seat for a hard lesson in cowardice as he tries to pass off his wife as his sister to save his own skin. Later we learn about loyalty when he rescues his nephew Lot from some shady kings. And then, most memorably perhaps, Abraham teaches us about the beauty and innocence of pure belief when God takes him outside for a midnight stroll one night and says, "Look at the sky. Count the stars. Can you do it? Count your descendants! You're going to have a big family."[1]

*Okay, God.*

Still later, after decades of drying Sarah's tears and mourning the vacancy in her womb and in their hearts year after year, God is true to his word and gives Abraham an heir. He's one hundred years old now.

Many people associate the lives of Abraham and Sarah with hope and promise in the face of infertility. Their story has become a touchstone, for women in particular, who wake up every single day under that same flat, gray blanket of sorrow. The fulfillment of God's promise to Sarah is a beacon (or maybe just a flashlight) for so many walking that agonizing path. Wanting to be promised the same promise. Believing that a loving God would not create this insatiable hunger to have a baby in a person's heart and let it dwell there, growing larger each day, and then allow it go unsatisfied. *Surely* God does not do this.

I have some good friends who are traveling this same road lined with confusing exit ramps and billboards:

Trust.

Hope.

Breathe.

Painful hormone shots. Frozen eggs.

Breathe.

Wait.

Hope.

Results. Tears. More hormones.

Pregnancy! Blood. Anguish.

Free fall.

Adoption?

Hope.

Breathe.

Hormone shots . . .

And in the middle of their own arduous crawl, they get to absorb the knowledge that every day babies are born to crack addicts who have no desire for them, and babies are born to women who already have eighteen children and a reality show.

Even animals have multiple litters while my friends' arms remain empty. Indefinitely.

As emotionally charged as their story is, I don't really know how safe it is for Abraham and Sarah to become the poster children for infertility. God made a specific covenant with them. It is not the covenant he makes with everyone. And yet, in seeming contradiction, we hear the psalmist say, "Delight yourself also in the LORD, and He shall give you the desires of your heart."[2]

I have no idea what to do with this. If I had gone to seminary I could probably shed a little light here. My friends, who cannot seem to have a baby, delight themselves in the Lord. Big-time. And still the most passionate desire of their hearts seems to gather cobwebs. I'd like to think I delight myself in the Lord. I'll bet you do too. Meanwhile there are definitely things I've prayed for fervently that my heart just has to keep on hoping for. Or letting go of.

Are we out of alignment with God's desire for what we should be desiring?

There's no easy way to discern all that. Maybe for others. Not for me.

What if the big takeaway moment from Abraham and Sarah is not about the delivery room at all? What if, instead, the lesson here is that the real work of faith—the real *point* of faith—happens in the waiting room? When we're stuck sitting in those scratchy upholstered chairs under fluorescent bulbs. Drinking lukewarm coffee. Flipping through last year's magazines and watching reruns of *Matlock*. Trying to stay busy, legs crossed with one rogue foot nervously tapping air in the rhythm of restlessness. All the while fixated on the door. Waiting. Watching. Willing the doctor to walk in any minute and tell us everything we have already decided he should tell us.

Seems to me it's in that dreadful space between dream and delivery that we are most willing to let somebody hold our trembling hands. And rub our shoulders and make a fresh pot of coffee. Aren't we at our most attentive and vulnerable there, in that aching gap that lives between the longing and the fulfillment?

And really, isn't a lot of life lived there, in the waiting room?

Even if our dreams come true, they eventually give way to fresh, new, impossible dreams that land us right back in those scratchy chairs, tapping a foot, watching *Matlock* and the door.

Abraham and Sarah's dream came true because God was dreaming it too. A dream for them, not a promise for all. Imagine, after the prolonged agony of waiting for Isaac, hearing his first cries splinter the black night of their sorrow, setting joy free. Imagine the tiny promised fist reaching up to swat at Abraham's scraggly beard. Imagine soaking in the congratulations and the disbelief and the whispers (once of pity, now of wonder).

And then, years later, when that love had grown roots so deep and entangled that they could not distinguish his blood and breath from their own, imagine *then* what it was like when God—Redeemer, Dreamer, Promise Keeper—tells Abraham abruptly one evening it's time to say good-bye.

Hands him a dagger and points to a mountain and tells him to take the boy and go.

My own personal answer would be short and uncomplicated.

No.

I'm sorry . . . but NO.

My parent's heart wants Abraham to screech in defiance: "WHO ARE YOU??? How dare you??? I don't want your starry sky! I don't care about descendants! Keep your stupid sand! I'll never ask you for anything else. EVER. Just please please please let me have this one small star. I'll die. I'll die without him.

"In fact, I'd prefer to.

"Please . . ."

Maybe he did beg and bargain. We don't know.

Reading in horror, all we know is the next morning he marches up that hill with Isaac in one hand and a knife in the other. And when he had bound the hands and feet of his son . . . his only, beautiful child . . . and placed him on an altar in the woods, only *then* did an angel of the Lord call his name frantically from the heavens.

Abraham! Abraham! Wait!!

The waiting.

The unthinkable time between the knife poised high above the thing you love most, the blade ready to plunge into your dreams, and the moment God calls your name at the last second.

Wait!

Wait!

Look! Something is stuck in those bushes over there . . .

To be old, to have lived fully, is to have done a lot of waiting. Waiting that pays off sometimes. Probably a lot of waiting that doesn't. Waiting to have. To move. Waiting to heal. Waiting to go home.

This past Valentine's Day I read about an organization in New York City that was collecting homemade valentines to hand out with all the meals that would be delivered to the eighteen thousand homebound individuals in that city. Think about that. Eighteen thousand people in one city who, because of illness or age or disability, can't leave their homes.

Medicine has to be delivered. Volunteers bring them every meal. If they're lucky, a family member or friend or pastor checks on them once in a while. And the best they can do is wait.

It made me so, so sad to think about those people. Sad enough to start rummaging through our glue sticks and construction paper and unleash my children to get busy making valentines to send to the Big Apple. Then it struck me that there must be homebound people right here in Tulsa. I made a quick call to Meals on Wheels and discovered that in fact about twelve hundred people every day depend on this service from inside their four walls. I realized these folks could be in my own neighborhood and I would never even know it. The lady at the agency told me that many of these elderly people do not have any visiting grandchildren and would treasure a valentine they could tape to the fridge. It would probably stay there all year long, she said.

My vision expanded.

My first idea was to collect some valentine-y art supplies— paper, stickers, ribbon, doilies—and distribute them to my son's third-grade classmates and get a few more valentines made that way. Then, like the Grinch, my project idea grew three sizes that day.

Now I wanted all the third graders in the whole school to participate. It's worth noting that at this particular school, *all the third graders* includes about three hundred kids. The size of this school is bigger than many small colleges. For the first six months, I felt like I was dropping off my baby at LAX.

"Go get 'em, tiger!" I would say. Then, watching him disappear into a sea of backpacks, I would try not to throw up. It's been a tough adjustment (for me, mostly). But for my little valentines project, the numbers were in my favor.

I made a mad dash to an art supply store and got the goods. The classrooms already had markers and glue and scissors, of course. I was up until 2:00 a.m. compiling twelve big packets of valentines supplies, one for each third-grade class. (A suggestion: never try to separate a stack of three hundred wafer-thin doilies, or you will grind your molars into a nice, fine powder.)

I am trying to act quickly on crazy ideas these days. I'm finding they are often the best ones. Lord knows I have a stockpile of safe and reasonable ideas to last until Y3K. I'm tired of doling out love in level tablespoons.

Even at two in the morning, I was super-energized as I prepped and packaged the crafts. I wrote a short letter for each teacher to read to the kids about what we were doing and why. And then I left them to cut and paste as much love as they could muster.

A few days later, I picked up all the valentines (bags and bags of them) and was planning to drive them over to Meals on Wheels. Being a little ahead of schedule, I sat in my car and made the grave mistake of starting to read a few until they were soaked and soggy with my tears.

"Dear Valentine. Do you feel okay? I hope you have enough food. Maybe this will give you enough love."

"Be mine, Valentine!! (Come on! You *know* you want to.)"

"If you're reading this, then you should know that you are loved, and I hope you'll be my Valentine this year."

And then, the one that sent me over the edge: "Valentine, are you sad? Would this help?"

Below the words was a teeny metal fake-ruby ring taped securely inside a purple crayon heart.

"Yours truly and forever, Timothy."

I closed my eyes and imagined someone else's grandma turning the calendar page to February 14 and swallowing a little more sadness, remembering an old sweetheart. Or a dance. Or a box of chocolates. Kept company only by her memories now, she pushes down self-pity and shakes off the invisible residue of loneliness that keeps trying to settle on her. She's hungry now. Lunch should be here soon. And so, just like every other Tuesday, she waits. And waits.

Unaware that Timothy's proposal and ring are en route.

Unaware that somewhere on the other side of Tulsa she is loved a little bit by a third grader and a forty-year-old stay-at-home mom, and the great big God of galaxies who knew her name even under Abraham's starry sky that night.

Today, lunch might be worth the wait.

*He took him outside and said, "Look up at the sky and count the stars . . . so shall your offspring be." (Genesis 15:5)*

# who but you
## *abraham and sarah*
### Lyrics from *Music Inspired by The Story*

Too little too late,
His time has come and gone.
Is that what they say when I walk by?
I've got a little more gray, my steps are slow and long
And the promise you've made fades in the moonlight.

I see a star,
You see the Milky Way.
I see one man counting sand
But you see generations.

Who, but you,
would ever choose to dream your dream in me?
Tell me who, but you, would dare me to
Believe what I can't see?
Who but you?

You'd think by now
It wouldn't bother me,
The hush from the crowd when I walk by.
And you'd think somehow I'd let my heart believe
It's time to let go of lullabies.

I see a star,
You see a galaxy.
There's just one hope, just one way
These arms will not stay empty.

So call me crazy,
Call me a fool.
You alone can do the things you promised to.
You are Yahweh, I'm just a man.
I'm counting tiny grains of sand,
Placing every promise in your hand.

*joseph*
# how to pray for a terrorist

I WAS WELL into my adult life before I really considered how many people on the planet are lugging around the secrets and shame of their own family history. Wearing it like a prison ankle monitor that keeps peeking out from the hem of their not-quite-long-enough pants.

Go ahead, it taunts. Keep on trying to live the illusion that no one has figured out how bankrupt your gene pool is. Sure, you might not be *technically* incarcerated, but we *will* find you, so don't be stupid enough to try to pry us off that ankle in a gas station bathroom. We're family. You=Us. Us=You.

My family name, while certainly not perfect, falls comfortably in some category of normal, punctuated with a lineage of German discipline, the blood of hard-working Midwestern farmers, and an ample passion for the arts on both sides. As a kid, I liked hearing my grown-up relatives talk about our name in the third person: "You know those Nordemans, stubborn as mules!" or, "Now you listen here, young lady, the Nordemans take care of their own!" Membership into this terrific club was pretty simple: get born.

My own childhood was pretty idyllic. And because things only really happen if they've happened to you, I had a great deal of trouble imagining that dark and sinister things took place under other roofs. Frankly, I struggled to imagine that not all mothers made crafts and read stories and played the piano for their children, and not all dads shoveled snowy driveways and said grace at the table and smelled like safety.

Issues like abuse, abandonment, and addiction or terms like *foster care* were touched upon only in movies or after-school specials I would never have been allowed to see. My mom (get ready) forbade my brother and me to watch *Leave It to Beaver* because Eddie Haskell was such a sassy pants to Wally and the Beave but then would always be so "aw shucks" to June and Ward, trying to butter them up for their car keys and such. The whole thing just stank to high heaven of deception, in her opinion. She and I shared a good laugh about this recently after she was done taping the latest episode of *The Bachelorette*.

For most of my formative years, I pretty much had friends who lived my same life and believed my same beliefs and whose parents upheld similar values to my own. It would have been a foreign and deeply unsettling idea in my young mind to think that people spend entire lifetimes trying to recover from the devastation of simply sharing the same last name with someone else.

Bending, but not breaking beneath the heavy yoke of a painful family history is not for the spiritually feeble. Ask

Joseph. I get that most people would associate Joseph's story with forgiveness and mercy. I don't know anyone who would dispute those central themes. But there is more to his story than sheer survival and a startling ability to look the other way. He is teaching us about rebirth at the bottom of a poisonous family well.

It must have taken a Herculean effort for Joseph to not only face and pardon his deplorable brothers but then to hook them up for life with the penthouse suite and Paula Deen's pantry. Each time I read that story and consider what kind of brothers would not only dispose of their own flesh and blood so savagely but then also allow their aging father to drown in grief for decades, it's pretty hard to stomach. That's the stuff of evil.

You=Us. Us=You. You're supposed to have his back, you morons. Not drop him in a hole. Not sell him into slavery.

Sometimes my irritation gives way to creative immaturity, and I pretend to give old stories new surprise endings. I'll read a Bible story with a totally fabricated wonder and anticipation about what's going to happen next so I can be rapt with excitement at the big reveal. (What?! Zeeebras? A rainbow?) Each time I try to pretend to forget the ending to Joseph's story, I secretly hope it involves the brothers having to hand-stitch fabulous coat after fabulous coat for him, until their fingers are bloodied and cramping from the embroidery. Each coat takes months. Once completed, the brothers parade their coats before Joseph for his elusive approval, when suddenly

Joseph goes all psycho-PETA on them, spraying fake lion's blood all over everything and tossing each coat into a deep hole. "Next!" he hollers cheerfully.

I love that ending.

While forgiveness is certainly a huge takeaway, the larger theme of Joseph's life, for me, is punctuated by his refusal to be defined by his reprehensible and fractured family. After such astonishing treason, he had every emotional right to harbor the kind of resentment that would make Dr. Phil blush. He could have let his heart die in that hole, even if his body didn't. He could have worn the bitterness like a fresh tattoo. Traced every stupid shortcoming and burst of bad luck right back to that event for the rest of his acidic days.

Who in the world would have blamed him? If pain is a limp, betrayal is an amputation. And you can't just will amputated parts of you to grow back.

So many people have allowed the pain of a wretched family history to etch their life-scarred identities into their foreheads. They enter the room apology first. If my parents hadn't divorced . . . If my dad wasn't an alcoholic . . . If my uncle hadn't molested me . . . If my brother hadn't committed suicide . . . If my mom had stuck it out for the fifth time in rehab, things would be different for me. I'd be whole and healthy.

We know these people. Some of us have been these people.

In no way am I diminishing the very real wounds we carry, especially those inflicted by the people who are supposed to cherish us most. But if we let it, the wound can become more than part of the journey; it can become the destination. When we believe that Wound=Us and Us=Wound, it's double-fist-pump time for God's enemy.

Not so for Joseph.

He made a very distinct choice not to wear his wound for the rest of his life. He was dealt a wicked blow, and not just one. But in the face of his circumstances, he made the decision to plant and grow elsewhere. He recognized that the sun and shade of God were smiling wherever he went, so he put down new roots. In a sense, he divorced himself from the gaping wound his brothers had left in him, a wound that could have defined him for life. And in leaving that wound behind, he created a great gap of time and space where healing must have trumped bitterness.

How else do you explain his reaction and almost immediate inclination to forgive when he saw his brothers again after so many years? A heart that was still nursing that bruise would have raged.

Essentially, Joseph made a new name for himself.

He couldn't deny his DNA. He couldn't erase the abuse. But he could attach a different lens onto his camera and start shooting life through an eye trained to look for the good and beautiful things of God. And God blessed him richly for it.

My dad and stepmom were conducting leadership seminars in South Africa several years ago. When asked which leader they most admired, 95 percent of the (white) participants named Nelson Mandela. One man shared that when Mandela was released after twenty-seven years in prison for his anti-apartheid work and was elected president, South Africans were braced for a bloodbath to avenge decades of inequality and violence.

Instead the president preached reconciliation and respect for all citizens, winning countless leadership awards and a Nobel Peace Prize in 1993. Talk about shooting life through a different lens . . .

I learned some much smaller lessons about different lenses after college, when I moved to Los Angeles with a friend to wait tables and eat ramen noodles while we sorted out our dreams for the future. This was not a milk-and-honey moment in my life. I was really broke and pretty lost about what role music should (or should not) play in my future. In a short time, and after a fairly bloody-knuckled campaign, Mayor Survival won the election and started kicking my dreams around like squatters who'd better pony up and start paying half the rent. Naturally, this really rubbed my dreams the wrong way. But we all needed groceries, so we did our best to get along.

So, in addition to my restaurant job, I started scanning "musician wanted" ads in the back of trade magazines. Answering one ad, I auditioned for a position to play the piano at a small and burgeoning contemporary service at a very large, established United Methodist church near UCLA.

They already knew how to do high church beautifully but were just beginning to explore a more casual service. This was way before we used the term *worship leader.* Back then it was called "play an instrument and hope people sing along." Which is not to say that genuine worship did not take place or that worship leaders weren't leading. They were. There just wasn't a corner office or parking space involved.

In my first audition/interview, I met with a committee, a delightful collection of folks charged with weeding out the unqualified initial candidates. I answered questions about my faith and my life and then played them a song or two. That was hoop No. 1. A week later, I met with two lovely women I assumed to be assistants or secretaries to the actual pastor who would eventually hire me or not. Hoop No. 2.

To my great shock, there wasn't another hoop. These two warm and wonderful women introduced themselves as Janice, the senior pastor, and Kate, the associate pastor. As in *the* pastors of the entire church. As in, not just in charge of children's ministry.

This was jarring, to say the least, given my own evangelical background. I'd heard all the common debates within our own ranks: sprinkle versus dunk, pre- versus post-Rapture, wine versus Welch's. But an actual woman behind an actual pulpit never even registered on my radar. It just didn't happen.

They offered me enough money to keep the ramen noodles on the table, and I graciously but cautiously accepted. I needed this gig.

To say that my time at this church grew and stretched me spiritually would be a fantastic understatement. Toto and I could no longer even locate Kansas on a fourth-grade map. I felt like I was driving down a steep, winding mountain road without guardrails and might just careen off some theological embankment if I took a turn too sharply. I knew we all agreed on the destination. I just really preferred my old seat belt, which fit much tighter.

The service I was helping lead was small and earthy and full of very diversely gifted people, as you might expect to find in LA. I dusted off my best Baptist worship choruses and was feeling pretty good about my musical contribution. Plus, I really liked the whole service each week. These people seemed very real to me. They lived an organic, imperfect faith, transparent and full. Noticeably absent was that Whac-A-Mole feeling I can get in some churches when the subculture/agenda/programs/politics can feel more like a constant smackdown than a gathering of lost pilgrims. I liked that this church was not trying to be Six Flags Over Jesus.

One afternoon, Kate sat down with me to give me some informal feedback. She was very affirming and encouraging about the music so far but wondered if I might have anything in my repertoire that was gender neutral as it related to God. As in, did not refer to God in the masculine. As in, songs that don't use the personal pronoun *he*.

If they had asked me to strip down on the spot and paint myself purple, I wouldn't have been more shocked. Until that point, I felt like I had generously accommodated a lot of new gray area that had previously been undeniably black-and-white for me. But this was too much. Everyone knows God is a dude. I mean, everyone *does* know that, right? Ah, the cringe of hindsight.

This is to say nothing of the small issue that the kind of songs they were asking me to find and sing literally did not exist in my world.

(I ask you, dear reader, to ponder for a moment a few favorite worship songs that pop into your head . . . almost all of them are he-fests.)

I must not have done much to conceal the panic on my face because she quickly (and with great compassion) explained their reasoning. It was not because they had some wishy-washy lukewarm center from which their liturgy had sprung. It wasn't because they had a liberal agenda and sought to undermine the whole of evangelical rhetoric, and it *most* especially wasn't because they were women who hated men. Janice was happily married with a lovely family, and Kate, though single, certainly wasn't carrying a male-bashing chip on her stole.

Their desire for a gender-neutral God in music was, she gently explained, that many, many people are unable to associate the very word *father* with the kind of love and safety and honor that we ascribe to our heavenly Father. There are countless believers and nonbelievers alike who limp through life bearing the wounds and scars of abuse and cruelty inflicted by a male family member, a very real ankle monitor and albatross that scream shame and secrecy every waking moment of their lives. To be invited to sing or pray to or worship our "Father, Father, Father" is, at worst, a constant reopening of this wound, and at best, a profound distraction in what might otherwise be a genuine experience of God's love.

It turns out that the rampart standing between some people and true worship of their Creator can be a two-letter pronoun.

(I wonder now if Joseph would have struggled to sing praises to God if his hymnal had offered only selections about what a merciful, loving, kind, compassionate *brother* God was.)

I had to really think about this for a good while. And I decided to consider that maybe God had me at this church for a reason other than groceries.

I realized that I could dig my heels into the familiar soil of my own comfy vocabulary and roll my eyes about those liberal West Coast Christians. Or I could embrace the opportunity to try (for the sake of actually *leading* worship) to release the grip a little on whatever pain the association of *father* might hold for some and forge pathways around that, hoping to point us to God's real heart.

I chose the latter.

You can't alter DNA. You can't undo the abuse. But you can attach a different lens to your camera and start shooting life through an eye trained to look for the good and beautiful things of God. That's the challenge I accepted. Change the lens and lighting a bit, not the subject matter.

I was right about one thing: there was no gender-neutral

music out there worth singing, in my opinion. And I had pretty much worn out "As the Deer Panteth for the Water" by week five. The deer was dead. So I picked up a pen and started writing. About this God I adore. About God's Son Jesus, who gutted me with his mercy and then rewrote my ending. Writing without gender or superlatives. Trying not to paint in tired and clichéd brushstrokes. Trying not to write with empty jargon that would limit or try to define God's indefinable Self.

I shared these songs with that small congregation each week and watched the shell of cynicism and the church baggage crack and dissolve a little on many hardened faces and hearts. Like mine. I watched people find a new vocabulary to sing to their Savior. It wasn't my native vocabulary, but that didn't matter a lick. God, being the actual Author of our language, knows a thing or two about translating it.

I prayed each week that God would be bigger than a pronoun or the absence of one. And I prayed most of all for those who had been scarred by their own father or had been left too devastated by their own family to feel welcome in this one.

I'm not sure God cares as much about what we call him . . . as long as we just do. Wonderful Counselor, Mighty God, Prince of Peace, Shepherd, Redeemer, Creator, and my favorite, I Am.

Less than a year later, I would sign a record deal, move to Nashville, and begin recording. At least half of the songs on my first solo project were written during that season and test-driven on that congregation. I didn't have the heart to tell the program directors at Christian radio that the new hit single they really loved was inspired by two women pastors who asked me not to refer to God as a male. Tomato, tomahto.

Not long ago, I attended *The Story* tour sponsored by World Vision. Max Lucado spoke some compelling and wonderful words about why we should consider picking up the small packet of information on the chair beside us to sponsor a child that evening. As an artist, I have worked with World Vision and sponsored children in the past, and I am a big believer in who World Vision is and what it does. That night I felt compelled again to pick up a packet; I tucked it away in my purse.

Later, at home, I shared it with my eight-year-old son, Charlie, to involve him in our sponsorship and in prayer for the girl pictured in the packet. From her photo she looked to be about his age. She is from Albania and has really short bangs, high on her forehead like a twenties flapper. We read her name together, Alkida.

I told Charlie I thought it was probably pronounced Al-KID-ah. He disagreed and said it should be pronounced Al-KIDE-ah. We went around for a while, arguing different pronunciations until it dawned on me that I might really be sweating the small stuff, so we went with Charlie's pronunciation: Al-KIDE-ah.

Unfortunately, now all my brain could hear was al-Qaeda, as in, our nation's greatest sworn enemy. Charlie, not knowing anything (gratefully) about the wretched chapter of terror this group has inflicted on the world, had no negative association with the name. But it presented an interesting challenge for me during prayer.

Because now every night at bedtime, I hear things like, "And dear Lord, please bless al-Qaeda. Please make sure al-Qaeda has enough food. Please keep al-Qaeda warm and safe." And on and on about sweet, beautiful, wonderful al-Qaeda, who needs our love and help.

Kneeling beside my son, half of my heart is trying to pray for a little girl in Albania, and the other half is trying really hard not to pray for a band of evil terrorists run amok in the world. I am praying with what my friend Marilyn Meberg calls a zippered heart, trying to compartmentalize the love of Jesus.

But Jesus doesn't do zippers. His love doesn't get snagged or hung up on names or events or pronouns or gender or color or fancy coats or rotten brothers or famines. Or terrorists.

His love doesn't even get hung up on the branches of family trees that bend and sometimes break under the weight of our painful histories. It's too busy at the roots. Where the soil is soaked in mercy. Where the living water of Jesus runs well beneath the seen surface.

◎

*Don't you see, you planned evil against me but God used*
*those same plans for my good, as you see all around you*
*right now—life for many people. (Genesis 50:20 MSG)*

# bend
## *joseph*
Lyrics from *Music Inspired by The Story*

I am not my family tree.

These are different leaves, you know;

There are miles and miles between my roots and what
   I'm trying to grow.

I am not the slave they sold,

Nor am I royalty.

I've worn them both, the finest coat and rags that
   barely cover me.

But there's mercy in the soil, mercy in the sun.

Learning to forgive what cannot be undone,

And what was meant to harm

Can't harm you in the end.

Stepped out on a limb I thought might break,

But Love said, it will only bend,

It will only bend.

I am not my past mistakes,

Labeled by some place and time.

Nor am I a trophy case

Trying to maintain my shine.

I have dreamed a thousand dreams,
Watched a grain in famine, grow.
I am not my family tree;
I have branches of my own.

Oh, does fate resign us to find shelter for our wounds
Beneath the battered roof of broken dreams?
Oh, but I will choose to stand in the shadow
    of your hand
And see what grows when Grace has sown the seed.

*moses*

# how to get unnoticed

YESTERDAY, I CAME this close to punching the dishwasher square in the buttons.

It wasn't him. It was me.

He was totally behaving, doing his part, getting the dishes all sparkly and being fairly good-natured about it. But we have been spending *way* too much time together, and I was starting to feel smothered and panicky. Load me, unload me, load me, unload me. On and on with the neediness, which is when I almost punched him. Realizing this was a tad irrational, I waited until no one was watching and kicked him discreetly instead.

I feel about my dishwasher the way some wives talk about their husbands who've recently retired. I come home, and he's just always *there*. Hanging out in the kitchen, making annoying noises. Lurking in the corner with that mouth that just keeps opening and closing. Dishes in. Dishes out. It's creepy.

I have never been a good housekeeper. And even if I was, I would still bristle at the term. It sounds so *Ladies Home Journal* circa 1953. It's right up there with my other favorite label, "stay-at-home mom," which instantly calls to mind some exhausted, disheveled shell of a woman, lurching along like a marsupial with a child on both front and back, accidentally brushing her teeth with deodorant. I so utterly resent that stereotype.

*Wait.*

*Shoot.*

Actually, "housekeeper" is one of the few titles that pretty accurately sums up the job description. I am quite literally keeping a house. Keeping it clean. Keeping it full of food. Keeping it organized. Keeping the cat away from the hamster. Keeping the peace. Keeping the people alive inside. Keeping the love of Jesus alive inside. Keeping the dust at bay. Keeping evil out. Keeping calm in chaos. Keeping my fingers firmly crossed.

In a valiant effort to restore a little dignity to the title, I've noticed a recent trend among some of my friends who prefer to call themselves the *manager* of their household. And I've even seen a couple of e-mails signed:

```
Sincerely,

Tammy Smith
CEO of the Smith Six
```

I appreciate the effort, but for me, titles like CEO only conjure up images of lots of busy bees tending to the hive while the queen dashes out for a quick mani/pedi and a shoe sale at Nordstrom. In my life, this happens not.

I decided a few years ago to step away from my career as an artist to stay home and raise my babies. I was having a horrible time balancing the mom/artist thing (I've seen people do it beautifully, by the way, but I'm usually only really good at one thing at a time). And I was starting to be just okay at both, which quickly landslided into being miserable at both. I felt God's full permission and blessing to step away from the spotlight and music to spend this season at home. I hoped he would give me different ways to use the creative gifts I'm supposed to steward, and he has. I'm grateful.

I tried doing all the emotional and mental gymnastics necessary to prepare myself for the inevitable whiplash that would happen when I hit the brakes on my career and was home full-time instead. I didn't prepare enough though. Not sure I could have.

One of the hardest adjustments for me has been the constant undone-ness of everything at home. I'm a list maker and a crosser-offer. When I had a full-time career, there were a lot of lists to cross things off of. Finish writing the songs. Record the vocals. Work on a set list. Practice with the band. Meet with my manager. Meet with my label. Get on the bus. Perform at the gig. Go to the airport. Go home. All of these activities have a firm beginning and ending. Even if I did it all over again day after day, there was still a sense of accomplishment when my head hit the pillow because my list had a bunch of lines drawn through it.

When you are at home full-time with young children,

scraping down sanity's cliff by your fingernails, you draw lines through nothing. Because the second you finish folding the last clean pair of socks and tucking them into the drawer, somebody drops their dank, smelly towel onto the bathroom floor. The minute the last shiny fork gets put away in the drawer, someone puts a dirty plate in the sink. The minute someone's belly is full, someone else gets hungry. And incidentally, nobody here gives a rat's rear about my autograph. And the pay is wretched.

Everything is in a perpetual state of undone-ity. And that messes with my happiness a good bit.

My friend Beki said recently that she woke up in the morning and immediately wrote down:

1. Have coffee

2. Get distracted.

And then she crossed both off and felt a sense of accomplishment right away.

I think that's why I acted out so unfairly at my dishwasher. I know he feels the same way. He never closes up shop or clocks out either. His hours are the same as mine, 6:00 a.m. to midnight. No time off for weekends, holidays, or good behavior. He never rests in the satisfaction of a job well done because it's never really *done.*

And I could write another three pages about how much deep admiration I have for people who have careers and jobs outside the home all day and then return home to everything I just described.

I decided awhile back to hire someone to help me clean the heavy stuff twice a month while I take care of all the regular daily stuff. Someone suggested this might lessen my homicidal leanings a little. I feel eternally thankful to be in a financial position to have that option; I know many don't. A friend recommended a woman named Carie, a tiny lady from India who speaks with that beautiful lilting accent and never stops smiling. Ever. Even if she's telling the saddest story and starts crying, she's still smiling.

I was unsure when I first met her because she's in her late sixties and I kind of felt like she should be working at a library or volunteering at the Red Cross or something less physical than scrubbing bathtubs. I laugh now at my concern. The woman has more energy than any twenty-year-old I know.

Carie immediately usurped my heart and has become a trusted friend and confidant. I've shared some very personal stuff with her, sometimes through tears, over cups of tea late in the afternoon. A devout Catholic and hopelessly in love with Jesus, she will walk out the door in the middle of mopping if it means she's in danger of being late for Mass. Carie is constantly reminding me how much Jesus loves me and that he knows I have a "goot hawt." There have been moments when I've considered trying to crawl up into her lap but was afraid of crushing her tiny thigh bones. I'm pretty sure she has this kind of relationship with all her clients, and it makes me a little jealous.

She's a part of my family now. Showering my children

with gifts and trinkets, driving by and leaving dinner on my porch for no reason, clipping ads from the newspaper she thinks I might want to see. She even reorganizes and redecorates (ahem!) when I'm not home if she thinks she can make a room a tiny bit more functional or beautiful.

I realized something about her recently. She doesn't really care that much about picking up after other people's messes or scrubbing for the extra gleam. Sure, it pays the bills, but her life's real mission is to serve people. To serve their hearts, not their floors. Her mop is just the vessel. Cleaning is the way she serves. Serving is the way she loves.

Carie is in my head a lot when I'm cleaning up after my own kids. I chant little mantras. *I'm not folding, I'm serving. I'm not sweeping, I'm serving. I'm not loading and unloading, I'm serving and loving.* I try that age-old trick of pretending I'm folding laundry for Jesus and not for my ungrateful three-year-old. I try to mimic Carie's smile, hoping it might morph into something genuine, but I always end up looking all crazy, like the Joker on *Batman*.

It's a funny thing about serving people and how quickly ego gets involved. If I'm gonna serve, I wanna serve big. Oprah big. I want people far and wide to know about my service. What it's cost me. How I've sacrificed. I'm gonna need someone to blog about it. And I'll probably require a publicist because there will be so many media requests for interviews from people who are scrambling to shine a spotlight on what a Servy McServanton I am.

But as it's been said a million times before, staying home and serving your children is a thankless, bottomless job. As my friend Nicole Johnson wrote in her poignant piece *The Invisible Woman*, "At times, my invisibility feels like an affliction. But it is not a disease that is erasing my life. It is the cure for the disease of my own self-centeredness."[1]

It's when I'm slogging through this exhausted state of *servitude* that I feel the strongest kinship with Moses.

A lot is made of his insecurity, his inability to speak well, and his awkward early fumbling as a leader. But the part of his story that lands on the soft floor of my heart is the years he spent as a stay-at-home mom in the desert with those children of Israel.

The next time you read the book of Exodus, pay attention to the minutiae, the monotony, the repetition of his instructions to the Israelites and their whining and complaining, their stubborn disobedience time and time and time again. If you read it through the eyes of a parent, it will wear you out.

We're hunnnngry.
We're thirrrrsty.
We're tiiiired.
We should have stayed in Egypt where at *least* we had *fooood. Duuuuh.*
Why is Moses taking so looong on the mountain?
We're borrrred.
I know! Let's party!

Let's make a baby cow statue out of gold and worship
   that instead!
(We're sorrrrry . . . )

After the harrowing escape from Pharaoh, after they see
with their own eyes the plagues God unleashed on their captors, after an entire ocean splits down the middle to allow their
safe passage, after *everything* God has done to demonstrate
that he is completely for them, they still can't seem to put on
their grown-up pants and do what they're supposed to do.

It's like Moses is running an Israeli preschool for decades
in the world's largest sandbox.

In Exodus 17, we read, "Moses cried out in prayer to GOD,
'What can I do with these people? Any minute now they'll
kill me!'"[2]

Sound familiar? Ever looked at your spouse, square and
sober, and said of your wee little cherubs, "I seriously think
they're trying to take my life"?

But even if this is how Moses felt every morning when he
crawled out of his tent to face his flock again, weary and bruised
to the bone, he just kept consistently doing what needed doing.

I marvel at his faithfulness. Climbing that mountain to
listen carefully to the words of God and then trudging back
down again to give the people more instruction they will likely disregard. He just keeps loading and unloading that dishwasher, sweeping up everybody's mess. He can't help himself.
Love and devotion do crazy things to a person in the desert.

I wonder how life altering it must have been to leave all that chaos for a few days and be in the holy presence of God, without distraction. I can't imagine it. I don't know how to respond to people who describe the time they spend with God so casually. I hear it a lot. From women mostly, I think. "I just spent the sweetest time with the Lord this morning, pouring out my heart to him and allowing his words of grace to fill me back up. I feel so refreshed."

It's some version of that anyway. I'm not at all discrediting another's experience with God; all are bound to be different. Nor am I making light of the description. I just don't have any context for it, because that has not been my experience. I've probably said similar things in the past because I thought I was supposed to or the moment called for it, but, more than likely, I was faking.

The closest I can get to a "sweet and refreshing time with the Lord" is a pretty patched-together prayer life. And even that sometimes feels like the first agonizing day of yoga class. Like, I cannot possibly hold this pose for three more seconds. It is no small feat to somehow silence myself and every last hamster on the wheel. But once in a while I find my heart pulled so fiercely inward toward Jesus it becomes useless to struggle against the lasso. It's nearly physical.

Those are the moments, those beautifully rare times in prayer, when I am least inclined to actually use words. I usually end up sitting in perfect silence, hoping to hear a voice that's not mine. Listening. Listening. Straining. Wanting to vanish into that tiny space where God and I can really find each other for a few seconds. A world where doorbells and deadlines dissolve.

I cannot fathom meeting actual God on the top of an actual mountain, ravaged by holy cloud and fire that leaves the actual skin on my face with a luminous shine. I have no category for that either. It seems so tragic that Moses has to come back down the mountain, leaving that rapturous encounter at the summit to start mopping up the juice boxes and changing everybody's diaper.

The last fifteen or so chapters of Exodus simply blow my mind.

As if chief captive freer/preschool director/mountain climber/judge and jury weren't enough hats to wear, God declares Moses an architect and gives him the astonishing task of building a tabernacle so the Spirit of God has a place to dwell among them. Literally. It's a blueprint so specific and particular in detail it's exhausting to read, let alone execute.

Make the table from acacia wood.

Use a seventy-five-pound brick of pure gold to make the lampstand.

The tapestries should be forty-six feet long with fifty loops on each panel.

Make bronze horns for the four corners of the altar.

It goes on for chapters.

After these instructions, God moves on to wardrobe. With equally tedious instructions, he dictates, in dizzying detail, what they should wear when they enter this place of worship.

And again, without question or complaint, Moses rolls up his sleeves and gets busy about the work of God. Without one pat on the back. Without affirmation from a single Bible study group or spouse about how well he's using his gifts.

He loved the Lord God with all of his frail and fragile old heart. He loved the commandments of God, many of which he had broken. His life's work was rooted in the deep and lonely pleasure of obedience. If he had been jonesing for validation, he wouldn't have lasted two days with that crew.

That's what I find most astonishing about the way Moses tackles housekeeping. He teaches me to let go of reciprocal gratitude or even acknowledgment. At the core of my struggle to serve my beautiful children and keep our home lies the core of my struggle with life in general: the unnoticedness. I want to scream.

Hear me!

See me!

Tell me I matter!

Mean it!

Notice, please, that I am painting something extraordinary here on the canvas of these young hearts and it will take me a long time, but someday it will really knock your socks off and God will smile, and then I'll say how hard it was but that it was really worth it. And know also that while all of that might be true, everything I just painted in the last twenty-four hours completely sucked, and right now I could really use a hug. Or a Snickers.

The south wall of the Sistene Chapel is covered by the life and stories of Moses. Originally there were eight panels, including the beginning of Moses' life when he was hidden in a basket by his frantic mother and found among the bulrushes to be raised by Pharaoh's daughter in the royal palace. Tragically, that fresco, along with several others, was destroyed in order to make room for Michelangelo's *Last Judgment*. And so today, the life of Moses begins on the chapel walls with his journey in Egypt as a young man.

Just like that.

My mother's heart shrinks at how disposable my work seems.

The one fresco that honors the adoptive mother who rescued him, raised him, shushed away tears and nightmares, and carefully shaped the man who would lead God's people out of captivity and into a new story was the fresco that was destroyed so that something more beautiful, perhaps of more importance, might replace it on the wall.

My pride demands a more full-circle moment. I want some nod, however slight, in the direction of the person whose sacrifice and blood and sweat are behind the finished product. I want some guarantee that someday my kids will point to me in the bleachers of the inauguration or the Super Bowl (or at least not from prison) and say, "That woman there is what made this moment possible." I want the champagne toast. It's only fair. It's been manna Monday around here for too long.

These thoughts are always a good indication that I am

serving the wrong master. With the wrong motive. Mourning the lost fresco, missing the entire ceiling.

For me, the turning point in this story comes when Moses hands me his greatest gift: his list.

It's the list of complaints from the people entrusted to him. The list of what must be done, day in and day out, in order to sustain a nation in the desert sand. The list of laws and decrees he must set forth, enforce, and mediate. The daunting list of God's specifics as it relates to how and where he must be worshiped. Moses crossed a lot of things off that list, and also left a lot undone.

Then comes the most tragic part of his story. The finish line.

After all he had done, there was no moment from the bleachers. The Israelites never got to dump the big cooler of Gatorade over his head and carry him on their shoulders into the promised land. He would be denied entrance as a consequence for his own disobedience (which, truthfully, seemed like a pretty minor infraction to me, but that wasn't my call). He would go through every agonizing labor pain, his whole life beading with sweat from the effort, and never hold that baby.

And he *knew* that.

And still his obedience remained unchanged.

His commitment firm.

His toil endless.

His patience infinite.

Somehow he understood that great things would be gained from the wandering and the withholding. He walked and served and died with the satisfaction of knowing a life well lived, a holy life, is not a list.

It is a poem.

A poem whose Author has hidden meaning and beauty deep inside the body of the whole work. A poem that lives and breathes and aches with personal promise.

Like Moses, we try to find our place within it. Our worth. Our selves.

Some days our lives read like a sonnet, and other days we feel like the misplaced apostrophe in an awkward dangle. But every day, we are woven into each line. And not one of those lines was meant to be crossed off.

*And Moses said unto the LORD, O my LORD,*
*I am not eloquent, neither heretofore, nor since thou*
*hast spoken unto thy servant: but I am slow of speech,*
*and of a slow tongue. (Exodus 4:10 KJV)*

# it must be you
## moses
### Lyrics from *Music Inspired by The Story*

I'd like to look in the mirror, without hiding my eyes;
I'd like to see what you see, why you think
  I'm qualified
To speak for you, O God, Most High.

Who hides a baby in the reeds of a river, until
    he's grown?
Gives him a stage and the strength to deliver his
    people home?
'Cause I'm tongue-tied, weak in the knees,
Must be something you only see.
If there's anything good,
Anything that's good in me,
It must be you, must be you.
And if there's any part of my shaking heart
To see this journey through,
It must be you.
It must be you.

Not gonna argue with fiery branches that speak
    my name,
Not gonna start taking backward glances from where
    we came,
'Cause tomorrow's holding our dreams.
But today I'm here on my knees.

O God of parting water,
God of falling bread,
If my words should falter
Will you speak instead?
You must see something good,
You must see something true.
It must be you.

*joshua*
# circles in the sand

IN MY EARLY twenties I was more than a little happy to see a few things grow smaller in my rearview mirror. College classes, my restaurant job(s), and my hometown, for starters. I didn't really have any direction or plan for my life, nor did I really have a dream. And I had stopped asking God about that stuff, for the most part. I was just ready to go do something somewhere. Somewhere *else*. (I look back on that time with some sadness, not having a dream. Isn't having a dream for your life, no matter how unattainable, some kind of universal requirement for everyone? Everyone in their twenties, especially?) Regardless, I didn't have one.

Life just sort of kept happening to me, and I would react and respond rather than initiate or pursue. It occurs to me now that I've always suffered from terminal safety. Dreaming big means potentially failing big. Dreaming small means things stay alphabetized and the bills get paid.

Another thing I did not possess as a younger person: genuine conviction. My whole life, I longed to be one of those people who really stood for something; instead, I always ended up just standing next to people who were standing for something. Standing for good things, thankfully. But I've never had my own cause or passion, per se. I've never had that charismatic quality certain people have that makes you want to sign a petition or demand a resignation or give your last dollar to build a mud hut for a stranger in Uganda.

It's taken me awhile to admit this about myself, but I am really more of a sheep, more of a follower, than a leader. I hate that. I want to be a leader. I've always wanted to lead. Not because I would be leading toward anything in particular, but leadership would afford me the chance to look back and say to my people, "This way, my people!"

And they would say, "Onward, fearless and skinny leader!"

There are still a few things left to address in counseling.

Initially, I attended a small private and very expensive Catholic university sitting high on a hill in beautiful San Diego. Arriving on campus with my own evangelical background, I had difficulty initially with the Catholic part of this scenario, but my faith grew in some unexpected and beautiful ways in the classrooms of my required religious courses and in the capable hands of some deep and delightful nuns. I could never have afforded this elegant school, but I had been awarded a music scholarship, so off I went for a couple of years.

It was my sophomore year, I think, when the appalling images of Rodney King being beaten like a rag doll by LAPD officers started splashing across our TV screens. Not long after that, a jury acquitted the officers in question, and the terrifying riots began just a few miles north in Los Angeles.

I completely freaked. It was the closest thing I'd felt to a panic attack in my life. Like many, I was appalled that these officers had not been held accountable, and then I was equally enraged at the retaliation unleashed against innocent people who were caught in the post-verdict cross fire. Pacing back and forth in my dorm room, I became consumed by hopelessness and could feel the red-hot outrage crawling up the back of my neck. I could not fully absorb what was unfolding on my TV screen and stood wringing my hands in distress like movie people do. Wringing and wringing.

It was the first time I could remember as a pseudo-adult feeling totally incapacitated in the face of injustice. By the images of Rodney King being pulled from his car, the images of Reginald Denny being pulled from his truck, the image of the enemy's shadow in the orchestra pit, waving his wand, the mad conductor. It was devastating and sickening. And there was nothing anyone could do.

Tearing ourselves away from the footage, my friends and I agreed we had to do *something*. We could not just sit comfortably on our trendy dorm furniture, passing around another box of Snackwells cookies. We could not stand by on the perfectly manicured lawns of this esteemed (and mostly white) campus and not voice our outrage. So you know what we did? This is so crazy. I can't even believe I'm going to tell you. Get ready.

We made really big posters.

You read that right: Posters. Big ones.

I mean, we'd had enough. We marched down to the store and bought poster board and markers and wrote things in big, puffy, purple letters like, "Justice for Rodney!!!" and "Give Peace a Chance!"

We sure did. Darn tootin'.

And then we walked right up to the big ornate iron gates in front of the lush botanical courtyards that separated the dorms from the marble fountain, and we stood there holding our posters, just daring people to say something about it. Begging for eye contact. Bring it on, rich, white, sheltered, spoiled children (not us, of course, the other ones).

We stood firm and unapologetically. And then, after about nine insufferably long seconds, I had no memory of who Rodney King was. What I did know was how stupid and lame we looked holding our posters while the rest of the campus passed by, chatting, flirting, gossiping, studying, and jogging, glistening and carefree. Did they not know? Was there not a television in the cafeteria?

Surely at any moment someone was about to ask, "What riots? What's happening?"

Then, being first responders, we would educate them about the horrors unfolding, and that's when we would march. Boy, would we march. And then Channel 2 News would pull up any minute, and eventually we'd probably be gasping for air, having stood our ground on the campus of Our Lady of Tear

Gas, and people would know that we really cared about something and someone. And that we were agents of change.

Breaking into my screenplay, a voice yelled from across the lawn: "Heyyy!"

*This is it,* I thought. *It's going down.*

"Hey, Nichole! Nuh. Way. Those are the cutest shoes everrr! How ARE you, gurrl? Study group for logic class in Founders Hall tonight at seven. You're totally coming, right? RIGHT??"

Mmmmhmm (smallest voice everrrr). "Yeah. Okay. Yup, see you there. Nope, can't chat. See you later." *No seriously, bye. Please leave now. Like now. Just go. Please. Now.*

A few minutes of awkward silence passed among the other poster holders.

Let's go, you guys. I can't do this.

Yeah, this sucks. We're out.

Justice for Rudolph, I mean Rodney. Justice for somebody, somewhere who should not have to endure one more moment of something, I guess.

Lying in bed that night, I was so embarrassed and depressed, realizing I had been the campus jester for about ten of my life's longest minutes. (Naturally, I needed to make it about me.) No, come to think of it, jesters are actually acknowledged and jeered. I was more like Casper the friendly protestor, invisible and benign. I was so embarrassed by my naïve assumption that I could, with a few friends, do or say anything that might right such obscene wrongs.

The experience left a very real stone in my heart. It was

an awakening. The world was a war zone, and I was armed with tanks of poster board. It did not (as it might for some) have a motivating effect, fanning the flames, leaving me with a heightened resolution to find a way to make a difference, come hell or high water. If anything, it secured my role as a sheep for years to come. Other people can hatch the battle plan, I decided. I'm perfectly happy as support staff. Have markers, will travel.

And before you try and let me off the hook by saying something generous like, "Hey, that's what youth is all about . . . You gotta *find* yourself first," I have to respectfully disagree. Because a ton of really important work is being done in the world right now by young people who are full of conviction and commitment. They have little interest in floating down a lazy river of beer on a spring-break raft. They care about much more. They're effecting genuine change, and not with posters or social media.

The world is full of impossibly young people standing knee-deep with their buckets in the world's toxic goo. Environmental goo. Emotional goo. Spiritual gunk. Racial, political, cultural, educational, fiscal, and social muck and mire. But these wonderfully alive people are not pausing first to find themselves. Bucket for bucket, they are trying to clean up messes they did not make but refuse to live with. Leading the rest of us ninnies.

It's exactly that kind of leadership that makes me have to confront (again) my own inadequacies. I mean, *leadership* is such a loaded word.

I tend to hide behind the familiar, traditional stereotypes. Leaders are larger than life. Leaders are loud and charismatic. Leaders are motivational, inspirational, and have impeccably high standards. Go big or go home, the leaders say. Dog the Bounty Hunter meets Martha Stewart meets Tony Robbins meets Saint Paul meets Judge Judy. People I would follow into battle but never sit with over a latte to swap stories about joy or brokenness. In the presence of certain leaders, you speak when spoken to. Chop, chop. As you were. Churchill and Lombardi get quoted abundantly.

I lug all of these preconceived notions of leadership to the top of the same pile where I lug all of my other junk that needs a good purging. The pile that sits next to my Bible. The pile I must dig through, discarding, protecting, comparing and contrasting, adding and subtracting, trying to find context for real-time moments juxtaposed with Bible-time moments.

This gets tricky in the leadership department. To be a leader, pharaoh, king, judge, lord, priest, or husband in Bible times pretty much amounted to you doing what you saw fit while the rest of your kingdom, village, tribe, slaves, wives, and children assumed a posture of submission. And still, there were good and bad, fair and unfair leaders in that cultural context. But fear mostly ruled the day, it seemed.

I think it's interesting that Jesus didn't really fit that leadership mold. Had we lived then, would we have said about Jesus, "Now, there goes a great leader"? Wouldn't the absence of fear and intimidation have somewhat disqualified him?

Apparently not. As we know, throngs of people followed him. Why? Because sheep know shepherds. Shepherds don't rally and roar or write books about habits of the highly effective. They collect quietly. They herd discreetly. They nudge. They rescue. Shepherds whisper, and flocks respond. Sheep know his voice. And his voice is a beautiful invitation, not a battle cry or bullet points from a leadership conference.

Jesus sort of topples the model of traditional leadership. He starts at the bottom. First things first. Let's get those feet washed. This is how Jesus leads. And it's why marriages and corporations and ministries thrive under his model of servant leadership. Stooping, not looming. Tending, not monitoring.

But the Old Testament leader was a different story. In order to enter the promised land, the Old Testament Israelites had to get serious about strategy. About obedience and priorities. And there was only one guy who was gonna take them all the way this time, and it wasn't Moses.

Moses, as I've mentioned, was a guy who spoke my language. He was nervous. Insecure. He had a past. He was weary. He wasn't a natural-born leader at all. Not by a long shot. He had a short temper and a long list of inadequacies. And he was wrecked by God's mercy for himself and for Israel. Moses didn't intimidate me. He endeared me.

But Moses died before milk and honey could gather on anyone's lips, and as I'm reading along in the story, I know I'm going to miss him. Especially because his successor, Joshua, is Señor Shock and Awe. Enough wandering already! Let's do this!

*Booyah!*

The book of Joshua is a tough read. Please don't choose it for your women's Bible study. *Please* don't choose it for the kiddos at Vacation Bible School. In the book of Joshua there's no way to sidestep or soften this violent part of the Israelites' story. It's showtime. God said he would give the Israelites Canaan—a forty-year promise in the making—although Canaan was already occupied and Israel was grossly outnumbered. Joshua didn't care about that small detail, and neither did God. So pretty much the rest of the book is chapter upon chapter of epic bloodshed. And not just army-guy bloodshed. Regular civilian bloodshed. Even Caananite women and children were slaughtered and, if I'm reading my Bible correctly, with God's green-light blessing.

I'll just pause here for an awkward moment of silence to acknowledge that I still have no idea what to do with all the Old Testament violence at God's direction. I think of a nice Canaanite family gathered around their hearth for supper. Did they know they were living under a holy curse? That their very existence prevented God's chosen people from occupying their own promised homeland? Or were they just observing the ritual of evening family time? Children. Stories. Bread and warm milk. Until the front door flies open and bloody massacre is wreaked on every household courtesy of Joshua and his God.

*Huh?* Is this the same God to whom I'm teaching my children to take every small playground-bully/dentist/math-test fear in prayer?

I'll pause here for another moment of awkward silence for my inability to segue out of that last paragraph and into a bigger, wider illuminating truth that makes us all feel better.

I got nothin'.

Whether I like it or not, this was how God chose to stage the finish line for his people. The people he had so carefully delivered from slavery at the hands of the merciless Egyptians. The people for whom he had laid a straight path of safety right through the center of the raging Red Sea. The people he had carefully guided by shrouding himself in a misty column of clouds during the day and a fiery night blaze in the dark. Dropping bread from the sky. Spilling water from a rock. Disciplining with love. Holding the collective hand of a nation until they were ready to occupy a land of their own.

Now God was ready to make good on his promise.

Alllllmost.

In this embattled book, Joshua, for obvious reasons, is lauded for his leadership skills. For his keen and careful discernment. For his fearlessness in the face of giants, literal and figurative. He's a man's man. And the buck stops with him. In a moment as important as this, he is God's guy. I try to think of what sort of leadership qualities a person would have to possess to be hand-selected for that job. The mental sharpness. The spiritual fortitude. The presence of mind in harrowing adversity.

But these qualities, essential as they were to his leadership, are not the ones that inspire and amaze me. It is not the ground he gains that gets my attention but what he holds back. I am drawn more to his patience and self-restraint as he waits on God for every next small move. Carefully crossing *t*'s and dotting *i*'s when surely everything in him wanted to explode onto the scene and have his moment. They were so close, so painfully close, to the land promised them, when God started handing out eleventh-hour instructions.

They had watched an ocean dry up once before to allow their safe passage, and now they found themselves on the shore of the River Jordan, where God began to give them detailed directives about how to cross yet another swollen body of water. Details about how the priests must carry the ark of the covenant. Details about the distance the rest of them must follow behind. And once having crossed safely, God continues instructing that all men (who haven't been already) be circumcised before they go one step farther. And then they all have to wait there until everyone heals. Next he instructs that a man from each tribe must bring a stone from the river bottom to build something that would serve as memorial of sorts to what God had brought them through.

Now, if I'm Joshua, I'm highly irritated at this point. I'm spent. I'm already pouting and kicking sand because, for the love of manna, I think we've jumped through enough hoops already, God. Let's just go and take what you promised us, and then we can discuss circumcision and the little stone altar thingie at the after-party. No disrespect.

This, oddly enough, was not Joshua's response. I see that as long as he is the leader, his first priority is following *his* leader. He questions nothing. He does not roll his eyes at the litany of last-minute instructions. He just keeps his head down and goes about the small and steady business of obedience.

Then, having safely crossed the Jordan and having carefully followed each of God's decrees, finally, *finally*, the Israelites can claim what's been promised them, right?

You bet.

Allllmost.

Just a few more laborious items on the list. The first one involves everyone's favorite activity, marching in circles. For seven days. Marching, marching, circling, circling around the walls of Jericho until God gives the signal and the priests blow their trumpets and everybody hollers and the wall comes down.

Poor Joshua.

It's almost too cruel.

I'm sorry, but is forty years' worth of walking in circles not sufficient? Could you explain why we need to keep circling for seven more days? Are trumpets really necessary? Can we please move this plan along without marching band rehearsal? I've earned it, God. You *know* I've earned it.

What was God doing? Surely this wasn't some final test of Joshua's skill or allegiance? Surely God knew by now that Joshua would bow his knee and his life to God's authority. I don't think his character or capability were in question.

So what would marching in circles around a city's wall accomplish, exactly, when all God had to do was huff and puff and blow the thing down already? But time and again, Joshua doesn't lead without listening first.

Not long ago, I was experiencing a full-blown crisis of faith. A crisis of everything, frankly. I would wake up in the morning, and my bowl of Cheerios would be in crisis. I could not hear, see, feel, or know anything about what I thought I knew of God's presence, and I felt like a newborn must feel three minutes into the world: cold, blind, confused, and shaken. Desperate for warmth and nourishment.

In these many moments, I felt the tug to go sit on my park bench.

My bench sits high on a hill at a lovely park. The same park where my kids swing and climb and run and splash when the geysers and sprayers are turned on in the sweltering months. But I don't visit my bench when I'm with the kids. I just glance at it wistfully, promising to return alone sometime soon. Sometimes this is when I cannot bring myself to go to church.

I love my church, but for months I could not find God there. Not in song or Scripture or Eucharist. But I could find him on my park bench, where I would pour out my sorrow and anger and feel him slide over next to me. Sometimes I would put my head in his lap, and my broken heart would take a safe little nap.

My hillside bench overlooks a massive flat surface that extends out to become more massive flat surface. Several other benches seem to sit around its perimeter as well, facing the same large vast area of flat nothingness. When I first sat on my bench, I thought it was a strange design. Why not some landscaping? Why not a rock fountain? Then one day my bookmark blew away, fluttering across the vacant space and, leaping up to chase it, I realized, looking down, that I was standing in the path of a clearly painted labyrinth on the ground beneath me. It had not been visible from my bench. But now, looking down, it was clear. The power of perspective.

I have never known what to do with labyrinth walking. (Well, Nichole, it's fairly simple. You walk.) I know, but what does the walking *do*? What does it accomplish? It's like spiritual hopscotch to me. What's the point?

Studying the tradition, I found that labyrinth walking is a practice that dates back almost thirty-five hundred years and is gleaned from many diverse and ancient cultures. I have friends who find great meaning and healing and clarity in the simple act of walking around in silence, circling in and out of the painted maze, meditating on God. Inhaling his name, exhaling the turmoil and small daily tragedies until they are left only with the soft sound of their soles pressing into cool ground and the voice of the One they can hear more clearly speaking in their minds. Circling. Circling. Circling.

It was hard at first. Actually, it's still hard. Getting quiet. Walking in slow, looping circles. Turning off the obsessive voices. One foot in front of the next, stilling my heart, silencing the desperate insecurities, releasing all that can't and won't be clutched and squeezed by my fat, frantic fingers. And when the walking and circling are done, I am left with the small but magnificent reminder that God orders my steps. In the circling, in the labyrinth, I align my heart again with God's own. He is in the repetition. He is around each tedious, uniformed curve. He is God. He is God. I am not. I am not.

In the circling, I wonder . . . Did Joshua have a knowing sense that Israel needed to march around just a few days more? One last reminder before Jericho's walls came thundering down, giving herself over to their siege, that God was God and they were not?

God was God. They were not.

They had not done this by themselves. Self-congratulatory high fives were not in order. They marched with the bones of the ancestors held high in reverence. They circled with trumpets, heralding not their arrival but God's faithfulness. Maybe they circled once more to remember that God can *listen* to the dreams of your heart when you are seated comfortably on a bench nearby, but he will dream *with* you if you will begin to walk. Even if the walking is in circles. Even if the destination is his name alone.

◎

*And the* Lord *said to Joshua, "Today I will begin to
exalt you in the eyes of all Israel, so they may
know that I am with you as I was with Moses." (Joshua 3:7)*

# bring us home
## joshua
Lyrics from *Music Inspired by The Story*

I'm a man in the land of giants.
I'm the cry of a thousand dreams,
I'm the shoulders holding a nation
High enough to still believe.

We remember the chains we carried,
Won't forget about the day we left.
Every heart still beats with hope of a promise made,
　　a promise kept.

Yahweh, oh Yahweh,
Bring us a new day.

Bring us home,
Lead us to the highest wall, every single stone will fall.
We have never walked alone,
Only you can bring us home.

No mercy in the high noon desert,
No shadow gonna block the sun,
Still covered in dust from all our yesterdays and days
　　to come.

Every turn is a new temptation,
You want to bow down to something new.
As for me and my generation, we'll serve no one but you.

Yahweh, oh Yahweh,
Bring us a new day.
Every teardrop in the sand, longing for a distant land,
    we have never walked alone.
Only You can bring us home.

You are fire in the night sky,
You are cloud by day.
We're calling on the name of Yahweh.

In seven days everything was made,
And in a week, it's crazy how everything can change.
Yeah, and we gonna march around this wall
'Til we hear the Lord's call,
Hoping life will never be the same.
So when your life is all a wilderness
And your darkest night is every one you took a breath,
All you know to do is follow, hoping for a new
    tomorrow,
Where your sorrows don't exist, and pain is put
    to death.
As we stomp around a seventh time
I anticipate a taste of what he says is mine.
Cry, cry, until you see it fall,
Till you look beyond a wall
And you see it all.

## ruth and naomi
# bridge and troubled water

I'M SITTING IN my car in the parking lot of a store I've never shopped in, in a city I've lived in for less than a full day. I'm also sitting in quite possibly the worst rainstorm I've ever experienced. Pepper is secured in her car seat, watching her favorite show, the same episode she has seen six times already this morning. It involves a yellow robot really bringing the truth about friendship. Specifically, how we should not bite our friends.

I was totally the parent who was never going to succumb to this mind-numbing, soul-stunting level of children's programming. No sireee. Just reruns of *Little House on the Prairie* or *maaaybe* Baby Einstein, but only in Japanese. I smile now when people without children take on the role of the outspoken professional child rearer. Because the very bottom line is, Pepper is happy watching this perfectly benign show, and if we're honest for a second, we really should not bite our friends. It's uncool.

I weigh my options: (1) Go home and come back later when I don't have to sprint through a typhoon, clutching a two-year-old. (2) Wait it out a few minutes until the storm passes.

I choose option 2 and settle in for more robot lessons in friendship. Option 1 isn't a real one anyway. We just moved to town the day before, and we desperately need the basics. Toilet paper. Milk. Something for dinner. These are not things you acquire only when it's convenient. You do not show up to anxious faces at home without the TP and shrug and say, "Eh. Rain."

But the storm doesn't let up. It is coming down so hard and so fast that even the most frantic setting on my wipers can't clear the glass for half a second. I wait and wait with no reprieve, grocery essentials mocking me from just beyond the marina where I've docked my minivan. Losing patience after about ten minutes, I decide we will make a run for it. If Pepper has to keep one hand around my neck and the other around my dolphin fin, we are going into the dang store. I am not afraid of a few puddles.

Once inside, I realize how stupid my decision was. We are both utterly soaked to the bone, wringing out our shirts and now freezing in the air-conditioned store. I can actually feel water sloshing between my toes and pressing up through the laces of my Converse tennis shoes like I'd been dropped in a pool. I mentally recommit to speed and precision in getting what we need. Pepper is howling now, sliding around in the child seat of the grocery cart, teeth chattering, her diaper pushed beyond maximum absorption. Turns out Huggies were not engineered for hurricanes.

This is when I hear him yelling first, and see him running toward me, second.

"Hellooooo there!!!! Oh my goodness! Oh my goodness! Hellllloooo YOU!! Hello, ma'am!! Oh my goodness!! I've missed you! Look at you! Look at your baby!!! She is so wet and still so cute!! Oh my goodness!!! Hellooooo!!! I've missed you both so much!!!"

And with these cries of ecstatic devotion, a total stranger with a nametag that says "Frank" throws his arms around me, hugging me hard and then swooping in to kiss Pepper on the cheek and hand her a balloon. We are both so confused and stunned we let him do it all without protest. I become aware at some point that people have paused to smile at the happy reunion for a few minutes before resuming their shopping.

I like to think that my codependency issues are really just exaggerated compassion. I was always the person in high school who warned the class geek that a practical joke was on the horizon. I would whisper discreetly as I walked by, "Whatever you do, do *not* open your locker after chemistry class," sabotaging the prank and exasperating the pranksters.

I can't stand to see people be uncomfortable, and I'll do anything to avoid it, including breech every last one of my own personal boundaries. So I did the only thing I knew to do. The only thing that came instinctively. Without thinking, I hugged him back even harder and said, "Oh my goodness! I've missed you too!"

I was not about to let Frank absorb the embarrassment that he had greeted (more like assaulted) the wrong lady with the wrong baby. Not on my watch.

Pretty soon, a store manager came by and gently encouraged Frank to return to his duties. Frank patted Pepper on the head one last time and went back to bagging groceries, still beaming and still waving as he walked away. "I've missed you!!" he hollered over his shoulder once more.

I realized, standing there, shivering in the pool of rainwater, that Frank was the first person to officially greet me in this new city since our arrival twenty-four hours earlier. The first and only. With bear hugs and balloons.

It took a few weeks and several return visits to the store for the full picture to emerge. Frank had some sort of developmental issue, and I watched him greet lots of people this way, especially the ones with children. It turns out this particular store intentionally employs people who might struggle to find employment elsewhere, which is why it has my business for life.

But, not knowing this, I tried to avoid eye contact with Frank for a few subsequent trips, making sure I didn't end up in his grocery line . . . until I realized I was the only one in the store avoiding him. Everyone else, it seemed, intentionally lined up to guarantee a few minutes with Frank. They were actually waiting for his hugs, for his "Hellllooooo YOUs!" as he carefully tucked the eggs far away from the bulky items.

My whole life, I have thought of friendship as a series of unspoken rules. Make sure you're a good listener. Don't say too much too soon. Watch out for the "me-monsters." Don't ask questions that are too personal. Certainly don't answer any. Read nonverbal cues with precision. Keep your heart safe. Don't bite your friends.

But in the secret corners of my bubble-wrapped heart, I want nothing more than to be the kind of friend who races in with balloons and cries of joy and thinks nothing of drenching other people in sheer delight for just having stood in their space for a few seconds. Without reluctance or caveat. Without weighing boundaries or expectations. Without risking foolishness. I've been blessed with a few friends who have loved me this way in my life. But while they might say other nice things about me, I'm not sure they would say I have returned that love with the same beautiful abandon. I think they might say I love deeply but carefully, and in an orderly fashion. Always with a keen awareness of the emergency exits. They might say my friendship is marked by cautiousness.

That's the kind of friendship that stands in stark contrast to the friendship of Ruth and Naomi. Their relationship has become a hallmark of friendship for many. It's probably the most well-cited example of biblical friendship, with Jonathan and David a close second. (This is not an actual statistic, for those of you following along at home.)

Women are the ones most frequently drawn to Ruth's story as we seem to be the gender more often evaluating and taking inventory of our own friendships, especially with other women. The Ruth 1:16 promise "Where you go I will go" has been the face of countless greeting cards, women's retreats, and songs. (I wrote one myself.) It's a promise that inspires us because it sets the faithfulness bar pretty darn high. It asks us to look inward and assess if we, too, might make such a selfless choice in the face of such a devastating crossroads. It makes us want to hold hands a little tighter. It helps us promise our hearts to each other, come what may.

In examining Old Testament passages, rarely do we have the patience to dig into historical or cultural context. We prefer the sound bite. We prefer curbside takeaway. (Please note the use of the pronoun *we* in this indictment. I'm such a repeat offender.)

At some level, I assume it's my job to find the sound bite. Being a decent songwriter is not about unearthing layers of information and backstory; it's about finding the short and memorable hook—something catchy you'll still be whistling an hour from now. This is a great goal for a pop song. I just don't think Scripture was meant to be read the same way.

It was a long time before I realized that Ruth's story is unbelievably complex despite all the greeting-card evidence to the contrary. It is multilayered with complicated cultural information that is critical to understanding not just her relationship to Naomi but also her "pursuit" of Boaz as well. If Abraham and Sarah have become the mascots for infertility, Ruth and Boaz have become the poster children for the weary Christian single.

There is modern-day Ruth-related dating advice aplenty. Feel free to Google it. You've been warned.

If you polled one hundred Christian women right now and asked them about the book of Ruth, I'd bet ninety-nine of them could quote some version of Ruth 1:16, but only a small handful could explain what a *kinsman redeemer* is or the significance and symbolism of the threshing floor. I would have included myself in that handful until very recently.

Spouting sound bites will always be easier than mining for accuracy. After we get past the well-worn mother-in-law jokes, the sound bite from Ruth and Naomi's story is obviously about sacrifice and faithfulness. After losing both her sons and her husband to death, Naomi is left to drown in a bitter sea of grief with her two daughters-in-law, Ruth and Orpah. She's so devastated she insists people begin to call her by the name Mara, which means "the Lord has dealt bitterly with me."

I have no trouble understanding this request.

Then Naomi announces her intent to return to her people in Bethlehem, insisting that Ruth and Orpah return to Moab, the home of their own families, which will be their singular hope for remarriage and survival.

(By the way, Oprah Winfrey was named after Orpah, but her mother spelled it incorrectly on her birth certificate. How you have lived this long without that insightful tidbit is anyone's guess.)

But Ruth insists on staying with Naomi despite Naomi's every effort to dissuade her. It will be a long journey to Bethlehem, and Naomi is not a young woman. She'll need companionship, Ruth decides. She'll need the care of a girl who loves her like a mother.

Orpah, on the other hand, reluctantly obeys Naomi's directives and returns to her own people and land, earning a bit of a reputation as the self-serving one, which I think is pretty unfair. She's really only following the cultural cues set before her. After all, her husband is dead. She would be a young widow in a foreign land with no future to speak of. Naomi has given her every blessing to return to her family for support and a new start, which is both an obvious and wise choice. Honestly, I can't imagine choosing otherwise.

I can even picture Orpah having a heart-to-heart with Ruth and feeling better about leaving, knowing that Ruth is staying. I don't know why she gets such a bad rap, but every story needs a villain, I guess.

Meanwhile I'm trying to imagine Ruth's Moabite mother waiting for her at the bus stop when Orpah steps off the bus alone.

She's where?? She's what??

She's staying. With Naomi. Not her mother, but her mother-in-law.

She's breaking all the rules. She's embracing a future as an alien and an outsider, without the protection of a husband, and in the company of an older, needier woman. Not exactly a resumé builder. Obviously she's not thinking clearly.

She's thinking with her heart.

Forsaking a second chance at a future, Ruth slips her arm around the slouched shoulders of grief-stricken Naomi and speaks the famous promise, "Don't urge me to leave you or to turn back from you. Where you go I will go, and where you stay I will stay. Your people will be my people and your God my God."[1]

Earlier this year I was a stranger in a very strange land for about half a day. I was traveling to Guatemala with World Vision and a team of dear friends. My plane was scheduled to land about an hour before everyone else's. After getting my bags and clearing customs, I was to wait for them to do the same. No problem. I had a good book and some pistachios.

While I might not fly as much as I used to, I would still consider myself a confident traveler at this point, even internationally. But there was a small insecurity lurking inside me about being a woman alone in a strange country and airport where I lacked a good understanding of the language. My memory of high school Spanish afforded me the equivalent of "*Más queso, por favor.*" (Although it did improve as the week progressed.) I pushed my worries down, however, because I would only be waiting for my group for a very short time.

Besides, I could always read the signs. The bathroom sign is universal. Red almost always means stop. Dollar signs mean currency exchange. I could follow the suitcase icon until I located baggage claim.

Sadly, there was no sign indicating that my group's flight had been delayed for six hours in Miami. Nor was there a sign indicating that I would have no cell service. Or one that let me know that once I exited a certain area of the airport I would

no longer be allowed reentry or have access to food or rest-
rooms, but instead would be contained in some lonely lobby
of purgatory with no information.

The Guatemalans knew this, of course, but they did not
make a sign just for me. The nerve.

I started twitching after an hour. Hyperventilating about
forty-five minutes after that. The plan was not going according to the plan, and I was like a child outside the Humane
Society pressed up against the glass, hoping against all hope
to see a familiar tail wagging back at me. No luck. And *no
más* pistachios. I didn't have the name of the local World
Vision contact or the hotel (I had saved them in e-mails, now
inaccessible). No cell service. No Internet. No way to find out
anything about anything. And *no hablo español.*

About that time a guy seated near me said, plain as baseball
and apple pie, "Are you waiting on that flight from Miami also?"

My heart leapt at the sound of familiar English. I heard
fireworks and Lee Greenwood.

He was from Guatemala originally but was now living with
his wife in Washington, DC, and was fluent in both English
and Spanish. Recognizing my plight, he spent the next several hours guiding me through that insane maze and helping
me find little chunks of cheese. He ordered lunch for me. He
showed me the restroom. He helped me exchange money. He
spoke with all the airline people, updating me on the status of
our mutually delayed flight. I watched his backpack while he
went to find a pay phone. He watched my purse and suitcase

while I walked around with the laptop looking for a signal. He led me through confusing crowds to the right elevators and back through the right doors. He sweet-talked security people so that we might regain access to certain parts of the airport. But his greatest gift to me was erasing my panic in being alone.

His name was Jorge. But I called him Oh Winged One in Robes of White.

Jorge had come to Guatemala for a funeral and was waiting on some childhood friends who were also flying in for the service. After hours and hours, and once he had confirmed the Miami flight was in the air and would be landing soon, he left to go to his grandmother's house. It made no sense for him to babysit me anymore, and I told him it was silly for both of us to wait. We hatched a plan. I would find his friends as soon as they came out of customs and relay the message about Jorge's whereabouts. This was the least I could do. He made me a little paper sign with their names (and actually showed me their pictures on his phone), and we parted ways with a quick hug and some laughter about our unlikely and short-lived friendship. We exchanged e-mail addresses in case something went awry. I tried to wash his feet, but it got awkward.

Finally, when my friends burst through the glass doors of baggage claim with open arms to greet me, the lost and lonely lamb, I was standing perfectly still in the middle of customs, largely ignoring their arrival and waving off their embraces, holding a sign above my head that read LUDWIG, LUIS or ERNESTO.

Of course it would come down to a sign.

I realized later I had broken every single international traveling rule: Don't talk to strangers. Don't eat the local food (you have no idea where that lettuce was washed). Don't leave your purse with people you just met. Don't give out your personal information.

I broke all these rules and more. I could have been responsible and guarded. I could have kept to myself, ignoring Jorge's introduction and kindness. I could have been far more careful. And I would have spent six hours in lonely, panicked fits of tears until my friends arrived.

After Jorge left but before my friends came, I was eating a Tootsie Pop when a young girl, maybe twenty years old, sat down next to me and started crying quietly. I froze. The internal dialogue began. *None of my business. Look busy. Don't make eye contact. She's entitled to her privacy, etc., etc.*

Then I thought of Jorge and scooted my chair over. I tried, but we could not communicate, and she just kept wiping fresh tears away. Finally, I remembered, *"Qué necesitas?"* What do you need?

Through hand gestures and tears I figured out she needed a few coins to make a call so her mother could pick her up. That was it. Like fifty cents or something.

I handed her the money, and after she made her call, she stopped crying and we ate lollipops together, smiling in silence. Both of us breaking the rules our mothers had taught us. Don't accept candy from strangers. Don't give money to them either.

But some rules were meant to be broken. Ruth knew this. And generations of her genealogy later, so did Jesus. Hurting people don't always need a lecture. Sometimes they don't even need to share the same language. Sometimes all they want is some company or a few coins or to share some candy with someone who says, I'm with you. Until the plane lands or your mom drives up or our Savior comes back for both of us, I'm with you.

Maybe that's why I find the most gold in the last line of Ruth's promise: "Your God will be my God." Why did I always assume that Ruth's God was already Naomi's God? They certainly seem like a close-knit bunch. Surely they sat next to each other in church, no?

No.

Ruth, I learned, was a Moabite, and from a polytheistic culture. Her gods were many. She was raised to worship a certain way, and so it would make perfect sense to return home to the familiarity of her childhood religion.

But here's where I get emotional. Even in profound grief, even after losing her husband and both of her sons, Naomi must have modeled, in her bitter brokenness, the kind of faith that would stir something in the heart of Ruth. So much so that she recognized the power of the true God. So much so that she was willing to forsake her roots and history and native faith and ritual, and follow not just Naomi but the One Naomi worshiped, even in sorrow.

Is it possible that Naomi is responsible for converting the

woman whose bloodline through marriage would include King David and eventually the Messiah? I think it is.

Suddenly, the balance shifts in the story. Ruth is faithful and selfless, yes. Naomi is distraught and somewhat helpless, yes. But Ruth stayed, not just because she had an unthinkably generous heart. She stayed because Naomi had something she wanted, a stalwart confidence in her God, even in her grief. And Ruth could not bear to stay away.

The story has two heroines, it seems.

This is not just a story about an unlikely friendship between two women. Isn't it about what we should all be striving for? To be so committed and so demonstrative about our confidence in Christ that people are still drawn to us, even in our deepest valleys?

I want to be both women. I want to be Ruth, who doesn't second-guess or hesitate but appears instantly on the frontlines of friendship the second the you-know-what hits the fan. Handing out balloons and hugs to the storm-soaked. And I want to be Naomi. Even on my knees, hunched over in agony and bitterness, still with songs of praise on my lips for God. A magnet. A beacon. A person whose life makes it impossible to walk away from in favor of greener pastures. A person who, although she can hardly summon the strength to walk it, knows exactly who sets the path before her.

Who is never too old or proud to hold hands. Or to hold up a sign for another weary traveler.

*Where you go I will go, and where you stay I will stay. (Ruth 1:16)*

# i'm with you
## ruth and naomi
### Lyrics from *Music Inspired by The Story*

Love is a hurricane in a blue sky.
I didn't see it coming, never knew why
All the laughter and the dreams,
All the memories in between,
Washed away in a steady stream.

Love is a hunger, a famine in your soul.
I thought I planted beauty, but it would never grow.
Now I'm on my hands and knees,
Trying to gather up my dreams,
Trying to hold on to anything.

And we could shake a fist in times like this,
When we don't understand,
Or we could just hold hands.

You and me, me and you,
Where you go, I'll go too.
I'm with you.
I'm with you.
Until your heart finds a home,
I won't let you feel alone.

I'm with you.
I'm with you.

You do your best to build a higher wall,
To keep love safe from any wrecking ball.
When the dust has cleared, we will
See the house that Love rebuilds,
Guarding beauty that lives here still.

Who can say I'm left with nothing
When I have all of you, all of you?
In the way you always love me,
I remember he does too.

*david*
# why we watch the bleachers

FIRST I WANTED to be a dancer. Then, in junior high, I wanted to be an athlete. Then, in college, I wanted to be a bright and rising star in the economics department, deeply passionate about climbing corporate ladders, which is what I thought my dad wanted. He didn't. Then I was certain I wanted to be a teacher. And a semester after that, a psychologist. Then, after I returned the rented cap and gown, freshly dry cleaned, I just wanted a better shift at the restaurant so I could sleep in every day and party every night with my new bartender friends.

Then I wanted a do-over for that entire decade.

Then, finally, I asked God what I should want because I was so embarrassed to even know myself and was also fresh out of caring. That's when I started to want what God had made me to want all along.

I wanted music.

Music had always wanted *me*, but the feeling was not exactly mutual. Music came so easily . . . too easily, which meant it couldn't possibly be a legitimate path, right? A career in music was for flaky and fragmented dreamers. Music was my hobby and my first true love, but everyone knows that hobbies and love do not contribute to 401(k)s. I was far too responsible to ever really consider being an artist. I knew musicians . . . people who drooled at the chance to play in front of fifteen people at the local coffee shop. People who walked around like idiots, scribbling song ideas onto cocktail napkins with one foot planted in a different reality. Always creating, always daydreaming, forgetting to shower. I found these people to be interesting and even inspiring for a few hours, after which I felt a deep and arrogant pity for them. (A little ironic considering my own babysitting and bartending resumé.)

I had a map for my life. I just couldn't figure out which vehicle was gonna get me there. As much as I adored writing and singing, for a long time I kept my gifts tucked safely in the glove box next to the Chapstick and insurance papers . . . just in case, God forbid, the Aspiration Police pulled me over and I had to produce something . . . anything.

People love to ask me exactly when I knew I was "called" to be an artist.

I'll let you know.

But first, I wanted to be a dancer.

I had an awkward stage that lasted from age six to nineteen. There was never really an okay time during that period to be in a tutu, but at nine years old, I remember begging my mom to enroll me in ballet class. I was always tall and awkward. Never prim and refined, not even a little delicate. Some little girls are just built like wispy dandelions. You have to suppress the smallest sneeze for fear of blowing them straight into Kansas. Not this gal. But my young heart was certain that a dancer lurked just beyond the jutting knees and elbows and enormous teeth. I think I must have still believed in Santa Claus at that time, because I remember writing him a letter and asking for all the ballerina gear. (The fact that I wrote *gear* should have waved a small warning flag.)

I learned later that my Aunt Pam was the one who accepted Santa duty and sent the whole getup that Christmas. Leotard, tights, ballet slippers, tutu, probably even bobby pins to aid my hair in achieving something resembling a ballerina bun.

Driving to ballet lessons for the first time was agonizing. We had approximately six minutes to make it from school to the dance studio, which meant changing in the car, a fate worse than braces. Once I had successfully wiggled into my tights, I bent down to try on my new ballet slippers. To my horror, and with a half mile to go, I realized they were at least three sizes too big and utterly unwearable. I had full-on Santa rage for the rest of the ride. He knows if I'm naughty or nice but has no clue what size shoe I wear? This will be my first impression? I'm going to begin my illustrious dance career wearing kayaks???

My mom, watching in the rearview mirror as panic began to distort my face, launched into full mom mode. She is a practical woman, always swift and speedy with pragmatic solutions, caring little for appearances or ego. I have both marveled at and loathed this quality at times. First, she handed me a box of Kleenex from the front seat and suggested I just stuff some into the toes of the ballet slippers to compensate for any roominess. Oh, okay. I'm sure the instructor will never notice the three-inch wad of tissue where my toes would normally be. (And then, maybe later at the carnival, I can wear an extra-tall Dr. Seuss hat in case I don't reach the height requirement to ride the roller coaster.)

With three blocks to go, and a crisis that Kleenex was not solving, she actually handed me a roll of masking tape next. Why this was at her disposal in the driver's seat remains a total mystery. She tells me to do whatever I can to secure the ballet slippers to my feet and reminds me that real ballerinas have beat-up shoes, falling apart and threadbare, held together by tape or gum or whatever is lying around on the floor of the Kennedy Center. I was a dancer now. Chin up, babe, the show must go on.

And so, while she drove, I taped and wrapped and wrapped and taped until I arrived at the studio and stunned my tiny Russian teacher by being her first-ever pupil to attempt a demi-plié wearing piñatas.

You would think that this would have left deep emotional scars. But truthfully, I have only vague and hazy memories of my own embarrassment. The memories that are crystal clear are of my mom's face across the room. Never apologizing to the teacher. Never huddling with the other mothers to roll her eyes and explain the mistake. Never shaking her head and laughing nervously at how absurd I looked. And moved.

And was. Her eyes were locked on me. All smiles. Thumbs up. Obviously, I was hands-down the most beautiful, eloquent dancer in that class, and possibly in the country. That's what I remember about being a ballerina for three months. How incredible I was.

Not long after I retired from dance, I decided I would be an athlete instead. My best friend, Lara, never met a sport she couldn't own in about five minutes. All of the other popular girls were jocks too. I had my doubts about my own athletic gifts, but seventh grade is no time for doubts. It just couldn't be that hard to spike something over a net or toss something into a hoop. Besides, I was not about to miss out on all the French braiding on game-day bus trips.

Practice (for some ungodly reason) was before school, pre-dawn. My dad drove me every morning and practiced with me in our driveway many evenings. He tells me now that he nicknamed me Spider Woman as I seemed to have an excess of flailing limbs, none of them making contact with an actual ball but still looking quite productive.

My parents enrolled me in summer athletic camps. Uniforms were purchased. Gym bags were carefully packed. All the while, they knew how this would end. They knew I could hardly walk up a flight of stairs without twisting an ankle, much less contribute to any sort of sports team. It didn't matter. As many embarrassing memories as I would have, scampering down the court in the wrong direction, hurling the ball at the other team's basket, that's not what stands out. I don't see my coach's head in his hands. I don't hear my teammates groaning. I see Dad in the bleachers. All smiles. Thumbs up. That's what I remember about being a basketball player for three months. How incredible I was.

I have two children of my own now. I know it's common to give all children a trophy for trying, even if they didn't win. And I know that many schools now shy away from handing out pass/fail grades to protect everybody's self-esteem. Kids come home instead with report cards that say, "Good Effort!" or "Making Decent Progress!" I am not a fan of this movement. After a certain age, you win or you lose. You pass or you fail. Your boss is not gonna give you a bear hug because, doggonit, you almost won the account.

My parents' fierce support and encouragement did not disillusion me. Their affirmation was not a faux trophy, leading me to believe I was a champion on the dance floor or the gym floor, when I was not. Deep down, I knew I wasn't a dancer. I knew I wasn't an athlete. But every moment of my life has been shrink-wrapped in the belief that I will always be celebrated for trying something new and risking failure. Failure was never an occasion for embarrassment in my house. It was more like a high five that said I was whittling down the options until I found something I was great at. Even now, having had some modest success in the music industry, their faces from the bleachers have not changed much. I still see tremendous pride in their eyes—pride that's not attached to my accomplishments but simply to my belonging. To my being theirs. To my very life and breath.

Being a parent myself now, this gift is not lost on me. I've logged some painful and beautiful moments in the bleachers already.

It always intrigues me the way we spin Bible stories for our children. I get it. I know it's easier to tell a story about cute pairs of animals on a giant boat and leave out the part about God drowning an entire planet. We prefer to think of Lot as the good guy who sheltered angels in a dangerous city, not the guy who got drunk and slept with his daughters. We don't dwell on Moses the murderer. We hurry to get to the ram in the bush (at least I do), so our children don't really have too much time to imagine Abraham tying his little boy to an altar and raising a knife above him. For young children, a lot of Bible stories are too complicated and violent and disturbing.

For their mothers too, sometimes.

At the beginning of my journey into excavating the humanity of these biblical characters, I was struck again by our insistence on calling them *heroes*. Heroes of the Bible. Heroes of the faith.

Really? I just don't see it. I know they did heroic things when God empowered them to and when they chose God's path and not their own, but to slap the hero label on some of those foreheads feels awkward to me, if not a little far-fetched. I see profoundly flawed men and women who got caught in the net of God's mercy and were wise enough to confess the blackness of their hearts, realigning their messed-up lives with God's plan about a jillion times every month. They have moments of little-*g* greatness only when they are submitted to big-*G* Greatness. Otherwise they are mostly capital-*T* Trainwrecks. Like us.

David is always on that "hero" list.

Ask a first grader about David, and he or she will quickly tell you about a puny shepherd boy who toppled a giant with a small slingshot and a couple of rocks. Yes, hero for sure . . . that day.

For all the political buffs, let's pretend the primaries are looming in the coming months and the candidate that all your conservative friends are backing has a bit of an iffy track record that includes sleeping with a married woman, trying to cover up her pregnancy, and then killing her husband. He also has a daughter who was raped by one of his sons, who was then killed by another one of his sons, which pretty much plunged his kingdom into civil war.

Thankfully, this candidate *does* have some good leadership skills, and the word on the street is that he's a man after God's own heart.

ROCK THE VOTE!

We don't like to think about *that* David. Try sneaking the word *adultery* or *concubine* into a worship song . . . it's awkward. We like him better when he's dancing before the Lord or carefully plucking smooth stones out of a gentle brook. There are Bible studies aplenty on the Psalms. We like the David who worships. The David who blesses God. Who cries out to him. Who searches for him in joy and sorrow.

Second Samuel, on the other hand, is kind of a downer. Lots of blood and rebellion. Torn robes and ashes. Deception and disgrace.

It almost feels as if we honestly confront all the evil in the real David, it might somehow diminish all the goodness in him and all of the righteous and honorable moments we've all but idolatrized. We want our children to be brave in front of their own Goliaths. We want our friends to be Jonathans. We want our leaders to be fearless kings. We want a hero.

But we don't really want David.

Here's what I think.

David knew who David was.

He had to stand in front of a mirror just as I do and face the honest reflection, however devastating. He knew his strengths. He knew his blind spots. He knew, as we all know, when he was standing in the sunshine of God's favor and when he was shivering in the shadow of his own sin. He knew how to love. He knew how to forgive. He knew how to lie and how to deceive and destroy. And he knew how to throw himself at the feet of the Lord's mercy.

The best thing we could say about David, or about anyone really, is that he was a child of God and he struggled well. We do ourselves a disservice when we make him the grand marshal of some holy hero parade and don't allow his humanity to leak into our own. Because it's there, in his humanity, that we, too, find grace for our failures.

Here's what I think: more important than David knowing

himself was that God knew David. Knew his strengths before he hurled that first stone toward Goliath. Knew his weaknesses before he climbed the stairs to the rooftop that fateful evening.

Nothing that happened on David's battlefields or in his bedroom surprised God. He knew where he would fail and where he would shine. He knew and saw what only a parent can know and see. He saw the vast landscape of the man's life when the boy could only glimpse a grassy hill where his sheep grazed.

God has no interest in labels. At God's party you can show up wearing a crown or a burlap sack and expect not a single compliment or insult because everybody has to walk in heart-first. God doesn't call anyone a hero of the faith. That doesn't even make sense. Faith is the opposite of heroism. Faith is trust and vulnerability at its most naked and terrified.

We're the ones who insist on calling people heroes—and then watch in shock and dismay as they topple off the towers we've built for them.

How did God feel about David's life? Easy. He adored him. He said David was "a man after My own heart, who will do all My will."[1] God looked at David the same way he looked at Adam when he said his creation was very good. David, like each of us, was created in God's own image and could not escape his Creator's adoration.

When the giant fell on the field, when the kingdoms fell in his favor, when his moral compass exploded into a fireball, when his children terrorized his nation and his reputation,

God was there in the corner of the ballet studio. There in the bleachers. All eyes on his child. Watching him soar. Watching him fall. Watching David dance in shoes that were three sizes too big. Watching him fall apart at the free-throw line. Hoping David would glance over and lock eyes with his Father's heart. *I see you, buddy. Stay in the game. Thumbs up.*

At the end of his life, David's last and dying words are recorded in Scripture. True to form, they read like a poem you want to crawl inside of and commit to memory. Here's how *The Message* offers his final song to life and death.

> And this is just how my regime has been,
> for God guaranteed his covenant with me,
> Spelled it out plainly
> and kept every promised word—
> My entire salvation,
> My every desire.
> But the devil's henchmen are like thorns
> culled and piled as trash;
> Better not try to touch them;
> keep your distance with a rake or hoe.
> They'll make a glorious bonfire![2]

David leaves us with a beautiful benediction about the guarantee of God's covenant and a careful warning about the trash heap the devil will try to gather for his bonfire. He knew both moments too well. And he knew that when God looked into his heart, he saw something that resembled his own, if only a little at times.

If there is anything more heroic to hope for, I can't think of it.

◎

*The LORD has sought out a man after his own heart and appointed him ruler of his people. (1 Samuel 13:14)*

# your heart
## *david*
### Lyrics from *Music Inspired by The Story*

It never was about the oil dripping from my head.
I never did dream beyond the pastures I could tend;
It never was about the praise,
Not about the street parade.
I didn't really need a crowd when Goliath fell down;
I never meant to woo a king with simple
   shepherd songs
Or hide away inside a cave, safe from danger's arms.
I never meant to wear a crown
Or try to bring armies down.
It never was about me and who I hoped to be.

At the end of the day, I wanna hear people say
My heart looks like your heart,
My heart looks like your heart.

When the world looks at me, let them agree
That my heart looks like your heart,
My heart looks like your heart.

I never thought I would be much more than Jesse's kin.
Who would ever dream a king would come from
    Bethlehem?
I know that I've crashed and burned,
Lives have been overturned,
But you redeem everything.
Yeah, even me.

Five little stones
Or a royal robe,
Shepherd or king
Doesn't mean a thing.

At the end of the day, I wanna hear people say
That my heart looks like your heart,
My heart looks like your heart.
Unashamed I will dance,
In your name, lift my hands
'Til my heart looks like your heart,
My heart looks like your heart.

*daniel*
# getting lost, staying found

IT DOESN'T SEEM to matter how well I think I have pre-planned my morning. It doesn't really matter if I've laid out the kids' clothes the night before or have a head start on breakfast or set all the clocks in my house ahead ten minutes to trick myself into punctuality. I still end up darting madly through the kitchen like a meth addict, emptying my purse in a frenzied attempt to locate my car keys. Accusing houseplants. Barking at my children to get in the car *NOW*. (Children who often are already in the car, seat belts obediently buckled.) I have spent a lifetime loathing people who are chronically late. And now I find myself not the loather but the loathed.

Such was the case one morning last summer as I was piling the kids into the car to pick up friends from the airport, running predictably and woefully behind schedule. My friend Shannon was coming with her two daughters for some fun in the sun, and we were eagerly awaiting our reunion with them. Winding my way out of our wooded, hilly neighborhood, I was trying to make a conscious effort not to let my speed limit reflect my heart rate. I really wanted to greet them in the terminal with bear hugs, not tires squealing up to the curb at baggage claim, hanging out the windows like Bo and Luke Duke.

On this particular day, my self-restraint served me well because as I came over the last blind hill, I hit the brakes just in front of a furry little lump sitting smack in the center of the road.

There was no avoiding it. The only options were to drive over the lump or get out of the car, move the lump to one side, and drive around it. Peering through the windshield, I saw, upon closer examination, that this lump had a really wiggly tail and a tiny, wet pink tongue. He was trembling and, I think, peeing on himself, if I recall. His coat was matted and tangled, and he was staring up at me with a reluctant hope peeking out of the one eye that wasn't swollen shut.

*Not today. Not today. Not todaaay,* I begged. This is the universal prayer of animal lovers everywhere who are physically incapable of looking the other way. We have no choice in the matter. Paralyzed in the presence of helpless furry things. Immobilized in the force field of some canine Jedi mind trick. I would have been late to my own wedding if I'd happened upon anything dazed or limping on the road to the chapel.

I stopped, of course. Picked up the trembling lump. Texted Shannon that we would be a few (more) minutes late getting to the airport. And then we headed back to the house.

Charlie filled a bowl with water. Pepper scrunched up a little bed of towels in the laundry room, and we promised we'd be right back. The poor pup passed out from exhaustion before we'd even shut the door.

I spent the rest of the drive to the airport and back trying to talk my son out of giving him a name. I explained that somebody, somewhere, was really missing him and we would find his home as soon as we got back. I was rightfully worried about his immediate attachment. Too late. Charlie had already named him Rex.

Back home with our houseguests, as we all (including the lump) got reacquainted, I decided I liked the name actually. This was not a dog that could have ever embodied a hipster name like, say, Owen, carefully nestled in between handsome Abercrombie-clad kids on a Christmas card. And he was certainly not a Jake, slobbering along a hiking trail in a Kashi commercial. No way would he ever tolerate some doggy spa either, like a Winston would. Winstons are the croquet of canines. No. None of that high-brow stuff for Rex. He was a dog that would make putt-putt proud. He was *such* a Rex. Good. Kind. Completely agreeable. Beyond friendly. Loyal and low maintenance. Not especially cute. Not ugly. Gentle. A little stinky with a grateful heart. Oh, and something was wrong with his bark. He didn't have one. He just sort of coughed excitedly. He was 100 percent all Rex.

If our eyes are the windows to the soul, our names are the marquee. After sizing up your handshake and your breath, your name is usually the first thing anyone learns about you. It almost always begins with a name.

Hi, I'm Jimmy Carter.

Nice to meet you, Jimmy. I'm Rosalyn.

Hello, I'm Elton.

Hey, Elton. The name's Bernie.

It's wonderful to meet you. I'm Martin Luther King Jr.

Goodness, that's a mouthful! Pleasure's mine. I'm Coretta Scott.

Both the penniless and powerful, the honorable and the condemned were all at some point wet, slippery squawking newborns in the arms of another who told the nurse what to write on the clipboard. For some, this might mean a lifetime of socially challenging moments thanks to a lapse in parental judgment:

I must have misheard you. I totally thought you said your name was Apple.

With his name enthusiastically agreed upon, Rex limped his way into our hearts in about a minute and a half. His eye was pretty messed up, so I spent that afternoon at the vet's office getting treatment and meds, insisting he wasn't a permanent family addition.

"Uh-huh," offered the vet knowingly.

The kids were delirious with joy in his lumpy little presence. I insisted he wasn't ours, trying to help them imagine how sad another family might be right now. I had to at least *try*, so after checking lost-and-found websites galore, I finally made some posters. Shannon stayed home with Rex and the kids while I dashed out to post copies, but in my heart I was secretly hoping we were the proud owners of a new (although slightly damaged) Yorkie.

I slowed down at the very first intersection armed with a roll of tape and a stack of posters, and right away spied a little boy about Charlie's age next to his mom, taping up his own poster to a telephone pole.

**Missing:**
**Yorkie with a hurt eye.**
**My best friend.**
**Please call us if you see him.**

I pressed my palm into my chest and winced. I approached them slowly with a determined smile, warmed at the sight of this sweet little guy still in his pajama pants, high on tippy toes, handing his mom pieces of torn tape. I recognized her agony too, the bags beneath her eyes, the forced hopeful, chipper tone. When I told them we had Rex, the boy literally collapsed to his knees bawling. Then his mom started. And just to be a team player, so did I. Then she almost snapped my neck with some sort of reverse full-nelson hug. I couldn't believe how I found Rex in such close proximity to where he actually went missing. Just a few streets over. He looked like he'd been hitchhiking for months.

They followed me on the short drive back to our house to reclaim their pup, where more tears awaited us. A different kind.

How does the same Saturday sky, tires making the same crunch on the same driveway, the same identical ending for two stories, spell such joy for one and such sorrow for another? How do two little boys about the same stature and size hold a wiggly ball of fur, and while one cries for joy the other stifles sobs? One lost but now found. One found but now lost.

To her credit, the mother recognized what this moment was costing us. She delayed her own celebration and instead bent down to tell Charlie what an answer to prayer he was. How God had used him. How they had prayed so hard that their dog would be safe with a loving family (in the middle of one of the worst thunderstorms on record), and God had used us to answer that prayer. Her sensitivity didn't mean much to Charlie at the time, but it meant the world to me.

There will be many moments in his life, I thought, where he will have to make a choice that will cost him some tears and maybe even a small slice of his heart in order to be the bearer of hope for another. And it will feel all wrong, despite its rightness.

As they were preparing to go, one of us asked what Rex's real name was. I honestly don't remember their answer. I know it started with an *A*. Atticus. Or Adonis. Something out of a Cormac McCarthy-meets-Greek-mythology novel. I do remember thinking that it didn't fit him at all. But sure enough, as soon as they said it, his tail started wagging at record speeds. He had tolerated us calling him Rex, but he certainly knew his real name. And he knew who he belonged to.

It stood out to me how hearing his real name affected my emotional attachment to him almost instantly. He wasn't ours after all. My heart had become attached to a Rex, not an Atticus, so that made it a little easier to let him go. In just hearing his real name, I could envision his life with that other family, could picture him sleeping at the foot of another boy's bed.

His ownership was clear.

When I began writing about Daniel, I thought of Atticus. I thought about allegiance and how critical it is to really know your own name despite anyone else's efforts to reprogram you.

I made a point in the previous chapter to comment on my resistance to so much hero worship ascribed to some of the men and women in ancient Scripture. I might have to amend that a little for Daniel. For me, he *was* heroic. Not for all the things he did (which are astonishing enough), but for all the things he didn't do. For all the compromises he simply would not make. For every time he stood at the road's fork and took the righteous and most treacherous path, clinging to the core of who he was and ignoring all the noise about who he was no longer. Maybe that feels heroic to me because I project my own wimpy convictions into his story. I would have just accepted my fate after giving it a noble college try.

"No! I will certainly *not* eat the king's food!"

(I'm sorry. Did you say taco night?)

"No. It is defiled! No, I say!"

(Meet me with tacos behind the palace in five minutes. Say nothing to no one.)

Daniel lost everything when the king of Babylon raided Judah and became his captor, taking the royals and the educated elite of Daniel's homeland, of which Daniel was one. The captive nation's fine, young, promising men were forced to serve a dangerous king and pagan gods in an alien kingdom. What's more, Daniel became part of a new educational training camp that King Nebuchadnezzar established so he could expand his empire with new and virile blood. Thus the king began building his future on strong young shoulders, shoulders that were meant to uphold Judah's Hebrew heritage. Daniel and his friends were not abducted randomly. They oozed potential and prowess and were no doubt considered a prize of the pagan king's territorial conquest.

We never hear that Daniel gets to return to his home. Imagine just vanishing around your senior year of high school. No phone calls to relieve your anguished parents, no FaceTime, no ransom demand someone might pay any day now. No hope of reunion to sustain your dreams at night.

Imagine being plucked from the security of a known life and herded off somewhere frightening where your devotion to the one true God is reviled and no longer admired. Imagine how much instruction Daniel must have absorbed over the course of his young life about the exclusivity God demands of our worship. And in an instant, that heritage and deep conviction becomes a liability to his very survival.

There are so many remarkable moments in Daniel's story. So many challenges faced. So many losses endured. But of all the things Daniel lost in his captivity, I think his name might have been the most painful. The Babylonians would have been offended by his Hebrew name. So the king gave Daniel and his buddies new names. Daniel will be known as Belteshazzar. His friends (once Hananiah, Mishael, and Azariah) are known now as Shadrach, Meshach, and Abednego.

It is not enough that Daniel loses everything he's ever known, but now he must part ways with the one thing no one should be able to take from someone else. A name implies ownership and belonging, and Daniel's new captors did not want him to be reminded that he belonged to another land, another family, another tradition. If they did not call him Daniel, perhaps he would not think or speak like a Daniel or believe like a Daniel or rebel like a Daniel. And, just maybe, he would not worship like a Daniel.

A name is much more than just a name.

I spent a summer interning at a nonprofit organization just outside of Washington, DC. My weekends were spent on the commuter rail coming into the city in an effort to absorb as much as I could of the rich history found in the museums and memorials. I spent an afternoon at the Vietnam War Memorial watching families, old comrades, former lovers, and young grandchildren linger in front of the massive wall. Dropping off dog tags and six-packs of Budweiser, Bibles, and baby shoes, mourning those who did not and will not return. I sat on the grass nearby and let tears of thanksgiving gather on my cheeks that my dad's name was not among them. He came home after two tours of duty in that war. I try and imagine how different my life would have been had he not. And I can't.

When it came time for the visitors to leave, many pressed thin strips of white paper up against the granite where the name of their loved one was etched and rubbed a pencil over the surface, leaving the name on the paper. If they could not have him back, they could at least have his name smeared in lead. Folded and tucked inside a jacket. Near a heart.

Names matter.

I also spent a day at the Holocaust Memorial Museum, one of the most sorrowful experiences I've had. It stole my breath. A physical heaviness seemed to press in on every molecule of every exhibit—weighing down the hearts of those of us who were there to honor and remember the unthinkable loss of lives.

I didn't sleep too well for a while after that day. I was lost in anxiety at the realization that this had happened *so* recently in the world's history. Terrified at the persuasive power of a lunatic few. Not at all convinced it couldn't happen again.

I learned about the tattooing system at Auschwitz. Prisoners who were deemed useful as workers in the camp lost their names to needles and ink that wiped them clean of their past and stamped them with just a number to represent their unimaginable present. Those who were clearly unable to serve in the camp or who were elderly or infirmed were marked for the gas chambers but not tattooed. Why waste good ink on a body destined for death? No name. No number. No identity of past or present, and certainly no future. I fall apart when I think of how the God of Israel surely must have whispered in the ears of his sons and daughters as they struggled for air through the fumes, reminding them that no one could ever take the name he himself had given them. *Chosen.* They still belonged. To him.

The attempt to erase Daniel's name was an attempt to erase his deeply held convictions. How much harder then was it for him to cling to them? When someone addresses you by a name that is not your own, how do you remember the core of yourself? How do you fight fiercely to uphold your beliefs and embrace the consequences that come with a knee that only bows to one Name? How do you not just shrug your shoulders and bury the memory of your former self in the graveyard of your past?

When I think of how much easier it would have been for Daniel to acquiesce and start over and redefine himself as a Babylonian, I confront once more my love affair with all paths of least resistance.

When I stood next to the Vietnam War wall, I said silently, *I will not let my heart forget your names.* And a few days later when I stood in the Holocaust museum in front of the shoe exhibit, a literal floor-to-ceiling mountain of actual shoes collected from concentration camps, I whispered the same promise. *I will not let my heart forget your names.*

This is a promise I can keep because, while I do not know their actual names, I believe my heart does, and it won't forget.

How many times did Daniel whisper this prayer about himself? About his own name?

Meanwhile King Nebuchadnezzar began to have nightmares. Panic-stricken about what his dreams meant, he demanded an interpretation from his astrologists, with the firm understanding that if they were not up to the task, they would die.

They failed, of course, enraging the king further and extending the death sentence to an even broader group, including Daniel and his friends. This sent Daniel to his knees. Asking God, *his* God, not the stars and moons and planets, to reveal the dreams' meaning so that they might be spared.

God granted his request and unraveled the mystery to Daniel, who shared the news with the king. The king was astonished. Amazed. And a little terrified. He honored him with a high position in the royal court over all the wise men. He lavished Daniel's friends with praise, incense, and distinguished positions. An eleventh-hour stay of execution. Daniel went from dead man walking to royal adviser overnight.

In both moments, in both fear and freedom, I can hear him whisper, *I will not let my heart forget my name.* Remembering who he was. Remembering *whose* he was.

But then the king built a ninety-foot statue and demanded that all people of all nations and every language bow and worship it, under the threat of death. Some of the king's astrologers got wind of Daniel's friends' refusal to bow down, and they turned him in. (They were no doubt nursing a wee grudge still.) This infuriated the king, and he prepared to make an example out them.

It's my understanding that a polytheistic view has no real issue with worshiping additional gods. The more the merrier, hence the *poly* part. This might be why the king acknowledged Daniel's God as the "revealer of mysteries" when his first dream was interpreted. The offense lay in the exclusivity, suggesting there is only one true God, rendering all other gods powerless and all other offerings meaningless. This was the ongoing problem for Daniel and his Hebrew friends in Babylon.

You know the story, no doubt. Daniel's three friends were bound and tossed into a furnace of fire (which the king decided should be extra hot—so they could be extra dead, I guess), and lo and behold, through the flames, a fourth guy was spotted too. Just hanging out with the condemned men in the furnace. Counting hairs on their heads, no doubt. Reminding them of their names. And his.

Again, the king was astonished. Humbled. Adamant that all praise go to the Hebrew God. And he promoted the men (again) to a high position in Babylon. More dreams. A banquet. A mysterious message written on a wall that only Daniel could interpret. A prediction about King Nebuchadnezzar's demise. And then the fulfillment of that prophecy.

As the saga continued, Daniel, having quite the sterling reputation by now, ran into even more trouble with Nebuchadnezzar's successor, King Darius. Again with the bowing down to a statue decree. Again with Daniel's refusal to compromise his devotion to his God. (Am I the only one exhausted by the royal short-term-memory issue here?) And again with the death threats. This time, as punishment, he was sentenced to walk into a den of lions with the assumption that he wouldn't be walking back out.

Once more, God protected him. The next morning, there was not a scratch to be found on his body or his conscience. He never stopped kneeling before his God, and only his God. He never compromised or blurred his allegiance. His heart had not forgotten his name.

Daniel both inspires and embarrasses me. The level of his conviction is astonishing in the face of such outrageous demands. As it is for a lot of biblical characters, it becomes almost impossible to relate to his circumstance. The things he faced seem almost like situations lifted out of a cartoon my son would watch. Thrown in the flames. Facing ferocious lions. Interpreting dreams for kings.

Where does that leave me spiritually? No one threatens me with death if I do not worship who or what they worship. No one tries to force-feed me unclean food that defiles my religious diet rules. My convictions do not leave my life in peril. I might lose a Twitter follower and, in turn, lose a little sleep, but that's about it.

I know this is not the case in many parts of the world. I am thankful to live in a time and in a country where I am free to follow my heart down any path of my choosing. Depending on our level of honesty, we might lose approval, but we won't lose limbs.

In an effort to find common ground with Daniel, I find myself circling back to the importance of my own name. God gave me several of them actually. *Nichole. Child of God. Beloved. Ransomed. Daughter. Forgiven. Seeker. Finder.*

It's when I find myself stuck in the middle of a road, lost, hungry, and exhausted, flea-infested, and looking at the world through my one good eye that I start answering to other names. *Failure. Prodigal. Naïve. Arrogant. Neurotic. Insecure. Angry. Nervous. Desperate. Hopeless.* And after being scooped up and rescued, cleaned and cared for, after a good meal and long nap in the safe arms of the One who knows me and named me, it is only then I realize how close I was to home all along. Just a few streets over. My heart just forgot.

*The king caved in and ordered Daniel brought and thrown into the lions' den. But he said to Daniel, "Your God, to whom you are so loyal, is going to get you out of this." (Daniel 6:16 MSG)*

## no compromise
### *daniel*
Lyrics from *Music Inspired by The Story*

Throw me in the ring, toss me to the flames,
No one but my King walks me out unscathed.

Feed me to the lions, throw away the key,
How will they deny who delivers me?
How could I love another?

My knees bow only to One Name,
My lips have One King to proclaim.
I will lift none other high, this is my one heart's cry:
No compromise.
No compromise.

Let them keep their gold, I won't be seduced.
Can't be bought or sold, I am rich in you.
How could I serve another?

Kingdoms crumble, rulers fall.
My God, you will outrule them all.
One King, one cry,
With one voice:
No compromise.

*esther*

# gravy trains

I WAS SITTING in the library recently trying to get some quiet writing done instead of competing with the Starbucks soundtrack. If there were any truth at all to reincarnation, I would hope to come back as a librarian. Wall-to-wall books. Hushed, whispered tones. Sensible shoes. Yes, please.

I was curled up with my laptop on a big upholstered chair when I saw this man in his sixties barge through the door with a certain look that said he wasn't coming in to check out a book. Sure enough, he throws his chest back in the middle of the periodicals and yells, "HEY, Y'ALL! DOES ANYONE HERE DRIVE A WHITE FORD MINIVAN?"

I watch a mousy little lady raise her hand hesitantly.

"WELL, ****! I JUST RAN INTO THE BACK OF YER CAR, LADY!"

She hurries awkwardly toward him to discuss the incident (quietly, we hope), and he keeps yelling like she's all the way across the Mojave: "I MEAN, THERE I WAS. TRYING TO PARK MY TRUCK, AND I WAS WATCHIN' THIS

REEEEAL PURTY GAL WALK ACROSS THE STREET, AND SHE HAD A BEE-HIND YOU COULD BOUNCE A NICKLE OFF OF, AND I'LL BE ✶✶✶✶✶✶ IF I COULDN'T TAKE MY EYES OFF HER, AND THEN *WHAM*!!! RIGHT INTO YER VAN. OH, MY GRAAAVY!" (Oh my gravy. He actually yelled that.)

Once I got my own snorts and giggles under control, I peeked up from my laptop to see several other shoulders shaking behind their books. I felt bad for the lady and her van, but boy, did I love how honest that moment was. That guy owned it with gusto. He yelled the truth for all to hear. A "real purty gal" with a nice booty had distracted him right into a fender and an insurance deductible.

Beauty, as the saying goes, is in the eye of the beholder.

No one really knows the original author or the exact origin of the saying, but according to the trusty worldwide interweb, it's pretty old. Plato expressed a similar idea in his writings, as did Benjamin Franklin and a good many others over the centuries. More recently, Miss Piggy put her own spin on it when she said, "Beauty is in the eye of the beholder, and it may be necessary from time to time to give a stupid or misinformed beholder a black eye."

I do think it's completely fair for a pig in a wig to have a little beauty baggage.

My own opinion is that there is at least some truth to the claim about the beholder's eye. For me, it relies heavily on how forgiving that eye is. Because when you love someone with a devotion that is bone deep, you intentionally blur your own vision. You make your eyes all squinty until their flaws and blemishes become blended and hazy. The more you squint, the more your beloved begins to look like a watercolor. You don't see as many hard edges and angles. You see someone in softer hues, blending and bleeding in a lovely light.

I've wondered at times if I could petition someone to tag on one more verse to 1 Corinthians 13: love always squints.

Of course, if all that feels too gushy and sentimental, you can arrive at the same destination by way of the treasured American proverb that says one man's trash is another man's treasure. This rings true for both lovers and flea market finds, it would seem. I was unable to determine the original author of this saying as well, but I think we can safely assume it was probably someone's great-uncle.

In a perfect world, we would all be beautiful, and not reliant on a few "beholders." That way more frogs would get kissed, and our true beauty would be utterly appreciated without disclaimer or expiration date. Nobody else would get to weigh in. Not the scale or the mirror. Not the magazines. Not the ruthless inner critic. Not the sinister box of photographs on the top shelf that proves there was once a skinnier, sexier you.

Today, in the world of beauty, we are mostly judged by standards we had no say in setting and have no ability to attain. Most of us really want to pass all the tests, or even just a couple of them, but we fall embarrassingly short. And then there are the women who, in my experience, make it a lifelong goal to hit the mark on the beauty bar. Constantly practicing the obsessing, the compromising, the effort and exertion it takes to feel all eyes longingly on them. To cause traffic accidents. Somehow, in the end, these women do not often feel loved and beheld. They end up feeling objectified and beholden.

Then, every once in a while, you come across a woman who sees the world through a marvelous and different lens, unhindered by any of the beauty standards that paralyze the rest of us. These are the moms who let their kids leave the house with two different shoes and three inches of bed-head. These are the women who regard toothpaste and deodorant as their entire beauty regimen. They have never waxed a brow or heard the term *Pilates*. They don't stand in the doorway of their closets, slumped in shame, because everything is so last season.

As far as the general beauty rules go, these women radiate cluelessness. You know if you've met a woman like this because you'll daydream for weeks on end about what it must be like to live in her skin. You meet her husband and fully understand the term *beholder*. You ooze admiration and disdain for these totally free people.

Because, the truth is, for the rest of us, beauty does matter. Beauty and gravy, evidently.

Once in a while I feel a little glum realizing there just aren't that many stories about women in Scripture that make me want to stand up and applaud. So I feel compelled to pay extra attention to the ones that do. The story of Esther is one of my favorites. Partly because it has all the trappings of a good Brian DePalma movie and more twists and turns than a Grisham novel. Deception and intrigue. Deceit and double crossing. Bravery. Scandal. A big reveal at the eleventh hour.

And, of course, I'm a sucker for a good underdog.

Esther's story is about more than bravery and conspiracy. It's more than a complicated thriller starring an unlikely Jewish girl who saves the day. It's more complex than its plotline.

And in the beginning, it's about a beauty queen.

For all the hard spiritual work that women do to avoid being sucked into the vortex of our cultural preoccupation with beauty, it's interesting to me that Esther only got the queen gig because she was exceptionally pretty.

Here's a quick synopsis about the start of her story. (Please don't look for this translation in your Bible.)

The king of Persia, being rich and powerful and prosperous, throws an epic weeklong party for his kingdom to celebrate his awesomeness and wealth. His wife, Queen No. 1, is having her own party off to the side, probably so she doesn't have to deal with Sir Drunkalot, who, sure enough, hits the wine too hard one night and summons her to his court so that everyone can see how hot she is.

The queen declines. She probably has a headache. The king is enraged and embarrassed and decides to make an example out of her to scare all the other womenfolk in the land from standing up to their menfolk. He divorces her and banishes her from the kingdom because she didn't comply with his demands.

Later his temper cools (i.e., he sobers up), and he begins to wonder if he has acted too harshly. (Whaa? Nooo.) His advisers step in quickly to suggest that his highness might choose instead from the latest crop of gorgeous young virgins, who will spend a year . . . *a year* . . . getting beauty treatments just so they are up to kingly standards, at which point, he can upgrade to the new model of his choosing. (Aw, true love.) It's pretty much *The Bachelor* circa fifth century BC.

Ultimately, the king gives Esther the rose, and she replaces the now-banished queen. Esther is more than beautiful; she's also a woman of virtue and loyalty and deep conviction. She is also secretly a Jew and has clearly been ordained for a much higher purpose than royal eye candy.

When God places her carefully at the center of a potentially devastating massacre and conspiracy orchestrated by the king's prominent Jew-hating adviser, Esther intervenes. She risks her life by doing so. And she does it batting her lashes because she knows the king is helpless beneath her spell. Go read it again (in the actual Bible) to refresh your memory. It's a great story.

*Spoiler alert: she saves the entire Jewish race.*

So why do I get hung up on that one troublesome part of her story? The beauty part.

It's probably because I've spent many years trying to pick the shrapnel out of my skin from the cultural war of unattainable perfection that has been waged within me every day since the seventh grade. Trying to undo damage. Trying to unhear lies. Trying to force myself and encourage other women and girls to divorce self-esteem from the absurd criteria laid before us.

Given this mission, the idea that Esther could never have wedged her foot in the door without her gorgeous good looks is kind of hard for me to swallow at first.

I contrast her privileged position with what Scripture says about man looking on the outside but God looking at the heart. With parables about the least of these.[1] There always seems to be such a built-in assumption that God prefers to use the lowly. The least likely. The castaways dangling on society's fringes. And I think the church has reinforced this too much, pushing young girls so far in the other direction, teaching them we should only be concerned with the condition of our hearts and not our hair. Trying to minimize our desire to be beautiful in an effort to combat the preoccupation of the rest of the world. But it doesn't work. The lip gloss still flies off the shelves. I love how many ministries for young girls have sprouted up that teach modesty, and not mascara abstinence.

Let's be honest: beauty isn't the bad guy.

God made it. He made us to long for it. To long for the sacred and holy parts of beauty that reflect our Creator, yes, but also beauty just for beauty's sake, don't you think? Consider the other senses. Is there a scriptural subtext beneath every pleasant smell? Do we feel shame when we wrap ourselves in blankets that are too soft to the touch? Do we feel compelled to come before God in a posture of shame and confession when dessert tastes too good? (Maybe don't answer that one.)

Sure, beauty can distract us, even to the point of sin and destruction. We can ram into the back of people's minivans because our appreciation has momentarily morphed into obsession and fantasy. But in condemning beauty in general, we throw a lot of babies out with the bathwater, in my opinion.

I had a print of a Modigliani painting that hung in my loft apartment for a while. The name of the print was *Large Seated Nude*. And while the subject is seated and maybe a little large, she is anything but nude. She's draped in flowing fabric that exposes the tiniest glimpse of the top of her breast.It's one of my favorite pieces. Nobody painted eyes and mouths like the great Italian Modigliani.

A friend came over with her young boys once, and I immediately sensed she was uncomfortable. She later admitted she felt it was awkward to be around the painting. Although acknowledging that it was beautiful and evocative and not at all pornographic, she said it just seemed to weird to see "half a breast on the wall in front of my kids." I'm pretty sure her kids never even noticed.

It makes me sad to realize we are sometimes terrified to appreciate the perfection of creation. I shouldn't feel conflicted about the attention paid to Esther's beauty. I should marvel that God used her perfect bone structure and pouty lips to get the job done. Because it was obviously a job he chose her for, a job she was ready for. He knew what he was doing when he made those lips.

I recently was reminded of how deceiving outward packaging can be as I waited behind a car in line for the bank's ATM machine. The money machine itself was flanked by a couple of those large cement poles sticking up from the ground that act as buffers, I guess, from goofy drivers.

I don't remember what kind of car was ahead of me. Something regular and conservative with four doors. The kind of car a math teacher drives or maybe a paralegal. Then I noticed a little sticker on the rear window. It was a small cartoon monkey in a diaper holding a bunch of bananas. Beneath the monkey was a caption that read, "Don't monkey around! There's a baby in here!" or something like that.

Now, I've never been a bumper sticker person. Mostly because I've never fully embraced the suggestion that whoever is stuck behind me in traffic might benefit from the knowledge that my child is an honor student or from my stance on gay marriage. I was a longtime holdout on Twitter for the same reason. Eventually, I convinced myself that it was a great way to network and connect about important things, so I signed up. Sure enough, within twenty minutes I was tweeting things like "OMG. Who wouldn't want *this* for lunch??" and attaching a picture of my chicken burrito. Only to spend the next two hours refreshing the page to read replies like "Yum!" and "You go, burrito girl!"

For me, bumper stickers are pretty much the grandfather of Twitter. And you may as well keep your politics and your burritos to yourself because a red light is not a long enough time to change my vote or my lunch plans.

Anyway.

I'm sitting behind the baby monkey sticker, and I started thinking about how truly sweet that idea is . . . informing the world that you're carrying precious cargo. If you've ever driven a newborn home from the hospital, you know it makes total sense. I drove like a centenarian the entire first year of my son's life. I was terrified, certain that every other driver on the road seemed to be auditioning for the monster truck race, ready to crush my hood for pure sport.

So there is something endearing about an unassuming little sticker that gently reminds total strangers to be extra careful with the contents of your backseat. Because the contents of your backseat have completely hijacked your heart, and surely that is enough to discourage anyone from recklessness. I like the idea so much I'm thinking of wearing a similar sticker on my forehead the next time I head out to the grocery store: Be nice to me today, because I feel fragile and the world is a scary place to raise children. And if my baby waves to you, please wave back because she is too young to feel rejection, and I love her enough to kick a perfect stranger in the shins if you don't.

It occurs to me that maybe children should warn the world by wearing a Mommy on Board sticker.

Meanwhile, back in the ATM line, the monkey sticker car was finally done with its transaction and started to pull slowly forward. Unfortunately, it didn't clear the cement pole, and I watched (and heard) as the car's side mirror made contact with the pole and bent inward toward the car. I winced and waited for the driver to back up and correct himself. He didn't. There was plenty of room. He wasn't hemmed in at all. He just needed to back up a few feet and try again.

It's hard to describe what happened next. It was like the driver wanted, more than anything in life, to destroy the side of his car. He repeatedly rammed into the poles, scraping the entire length of his car as he drove by, backing up, re-scraping, ramming again, breaking the mirror completely off, backing up once more, followed by more scraping, more denting. It was just so strange.

Everyone in the parking lot stopped cold and stared, and I just sat behind him with my hand over my mouth in disbelief. If my daughter hadn't been in the car, I would have probably jumped out to make sure the driver wasn't having a stroke or something serious. Or that he wasn't a first grader cutting class and sitting on a phone book.

The entire side of the car was being destroyed. Over and over again. Eventually, he drove off, and as he pulled out of the parking lot, he misjudged the curb and ended up halfway on the sidewalk before he peeled out.

I sat there fairly stunned for a few minutes. Trying to un-ravel the mystery of why anyone would wrap a car around the pole of an ATM on purpose. And then I thought of that monkey sticker and broke out in a cold sweat. Clearly who-ever was behind the wheel was not in any condition to have a baby on board. I prayed fervently that the baby was at home with Grandma. It haunted me all day, and I still find myself looking for that car when I'm out running errands or in line at the same ATM machine, trying to make sense of it.

Ultimately, what we advertise on our rear windows (or our bumpers or our foreheads) is not always an accurate indication of what's behind the wheel. Is this not true for our personal appearance as well? We assume beautiful people are shallow because we've been told that beauty is skin-deep. In fact, if we're honest, we resent beautiful people because somehow we feel diminished and inadequate in their presence. On the other hand, we assume that unbeautiful people (it felt wrong to type *ugly*) are deep and introspective and have a good solid character because they've had to muddle through life without the benefit of perfect teeth. We always whoop and holler when the average-looking Joe wins *American Idol.* Or wins anything. Because then we win too. We guffaw when the supermodel trips on the runway because, seriously, she really had it comin'.

Esther reminds us to unlock the door and walk boldly into the room with whatever God gave us. Not to manipulate. But to serve. Not to grandstand. But to give everything.

I learned this from a third-grade teacher recently. I am the homeroom mom for my son's class this year, and his teacher (and I do not exaggerate) is Demi Moore's much prettier twin (which I realize is a physical impossibility). But I'm not joking. She is absolutely drop-dead-on-the-floor gorgeous. And, I would add, I have not had a lick of trouble getting any classroom participation from dads this year.

When I met her, I instantly felt familiar inadequacy issues rise up the back of my neck. Knowing I would see her often through the year, probably wearing a stain from breakfast on my shirt and balancing cupcakes in one arm and a three-year-old in the other. Knowing I would feel insecure. Chubby. Lame.

But now I don't really see her staggering beauty anymore at all. Because I have seen her heart, and it is so big and so stunning that it overshadows her perfect face. She rules her subjects with grace and honesty and integrity and an ocean of love. She rules with integrity and deep care over those third graders. She reigns with compassion and kindness but firm conviction. She was born, like Esther, for such a time as this.

Take a good look at your kingdom, and not your mirror.

Weren't we all?

*Who knows if perhaps you were made queen for just such a time as this? (Esther 4:14 NLT)*

## born for this
### *esther*
Lyrics from *Music Inspired by The Story*

Feels like I've been holding my breath
Trying to still my restless heart.
Everything hangs on my next step,
Finding my nerve, playing my part.

I found shelter underneath his crown,
Found favor inside his eyes,
Rock this boat, and I just might drown.
Honesty seems to come with a price;
There's a time to hold your tongue,
Time to keep your head down.
There's a time but it's not now.

Sometimes you gotta go, uninvited,
Sometimes you gotta speak when you don't have
   the floor.
Sometimes you gotta move, when everybody else
   says you should stay,
No way, no, not today.
You gotta ask, if you want an answer.
Sometimes you gotta stand apart from the crowd
Long before your heart could run the risk.
You were born for this.

I'm leaning on the ones before me,
My father's father's dreams.
I'm standing on the top of their shoulders
Calling the one delivering me.

One step,
One move,
Born to trust you,
Made to lay my life before you.

*job*

# when to make soup

I AM DEEPLY drawn to certain men and women of the Bible who have shaped Scripture with their lives and stories. Moses, for one. And Mary. Jonah, in moments. Thomas, for sure. Maybe I have experienced similar struggles or prayed the same prayers, hoped for the same sorts of victories that mark the pages of their lives.

Funny, though, how I seem to be equally uneasy about others. I was going to use the word *repelled*, but that's too strong. I wish *undrawn* were a word. I could say I tend to be drawn to some and undrawn to others. Perhaps these characters' stories hit a little too close to home. Or maybe I'm judging a certain weakness or, in some cases, simply a personality. I confess to having projected myself into the occasional biblical scene where I'm whispering to my imaginary Jewish roommate, "Listen, if Paul calls and wants to grab coffee, just tell him I'm not here but that you gave me the message . . . I mean, that guy is waay-haay too intense." And then I realize how ridiculous that scenario is, because Paul would never want to grab coffee, what with my being a woman and all.

(I have a few teensy Paul issues. There. I said it.)

This doesn't hinder me too much from gaining meaningful truth and insight from these folks I am undrawn to. I'm just trying to be honest in admitting that if I were to happen upon some of these folks in a store, library, pub, church, or family reunion, we might not be immediate friends. No offense. I'm sure they would likely say the same about me.

This nudges me toward a small confession: I avoid the book of Job like the plague. (No pun intended.) I know I am supposed to feel deeply challenged and convicted by the depth of his unwavering faith in the face of so many unthinkable tragedies, but honestly, I can barely read it. I would probably never sign up to participate in a Job Bible study. I don't ever quote Job verses. If my pastor announces he will be doing a sermon series on Job for the month, I will likely plan on mailing in my tithe check for the next four weeks.

It's too unsettling. Job's story leaves too many terrifying and exposed loose ends in my heart. Way too many confusing questions. Very few acceptable explanations. Unthinkable, unimaginable sorrow. All of his livelihood, all the fruit of his life's work, gone in a flash. His beautiful offspring dead in a blink. His physical body tormented by decay and disease overnight.

Oddly enough, for all the annihilation, God decides to spare Job's wife and his friends, who do not exactly rise up and meet him with the gift of encouragement.

It is then, as we know, in the face of this tsunami of pain, that Job takes an extraordinary and nearly absurd high road and lifts his head from his suffering to offer to God what he believes God still deserves: his praise. It is fragmented and threadbare but praise nonetheless. He offers this worship from a hollow heart and with a dry mouth on a mound of bitter, dirt-soaked tears. His worship rises up from the stench of his own oozing skin, which peers out from beneath the shirt he has shredded in his mad anguish.

Job models what no one should ever be expected to model. Tearing out a page from the *Hell on Earth* handbook and exposing the extraordinary heart of a man who is somehow able to whisper blessings into the blackest night and not be startled by the sound of his own small voice bouncing around in sorrow's echo chamber.

I have so much trouble absorbing Job's choice to bless God from the lowest place in the landfill because it means confronting the very real possibility that God would allow this to happen to me as well.

I already have fatalistic tendencies. I already live in a fair amount of fear that the hammer is about to drop at any second. If the phone rings after 10:00 p.m., I've already begun mentally laying out clothes for someone's funeral before I even answer it. You wouldn't believe how many ridiculous texts I've sent from an airport runway because the weather is a little too turbulent for my comfort level. "Just wanted you to know I love you. You will go on to do amazing things. I should have apologized for that one fight in the eighth grade. I was such a horse's you-know-what. Godspeed, younger brother. Until the other side . . ."

The reply is usually something like, "Yeah. Okay. See you at baggage claim, freak show."

I think because I have never experienced the catastrophic soul siege of loss, I pretty much constantly feel like I'm over-due at any minute.

My other difficulty in reading the book of Job is that there is no shortage of well-meaning crazies who have made a twisted theological mess out of the idea that God only blesses righteous people and reserves the most severe punishment for the wicked. They are desperate to connect the dots between AIDS or Hurricane Katrina or 9/11 to God's sweeping holy hand of judgment. What, then, do we do with Job? How do we reconcile what a good and gracious God will let happen to a person who has been faithful, obedient, and lived a lifetime of integrity?

Am I the only one terrified by this?

I seem to hold two beliefs in my heart at all times. First, that I am totally safe and carefully held in the loving hands of my Father. Also, that I am really not.

I first realized I had Job issues in my early twenties when I attended a church where the pastor liked to do this little verbal affirmation thing with the congregation almost every Sunday. Perhaps you've heard it.

Pastor: God is good . . .

People: All the time!

Pastor: And all the time . . .

People: God is good!

Pastor: Now, turn to your neighbors and tell them that God is good this morning . . .

Why in the world would I have a problem with that? Without a doubt, both pastor and pew were echoing truth. God is indeed good. All the time. It's impossible for God to be otherwise.

But there it was, stuck in my throat. At first, I tried to chant along enthusiastically with everyone else, but then I started finding an excuse to put a mint in my mouth or blow my nose at the moment of participation. Why? Did I fear I was taking part in some emotionally manipulated pep rally? Was this merely the churchy equivalent of "We've got spirit, yes we do . . ." and I was just resisting my part of the human wave as it rippled through the bleachers?

(I have teensy authority issues too. There. I said it.)

I don't think so. I think I resisted because of my acute awareness that there were people in that congregation who were sitting cross-legged in piles of ashes, barely able to lift their heads. Parents who had held a dead child. Men who had walked in on their wives in the arms of another. A wife who had suffered years of abuse at the hands of her husband. Owners of homes that had gone up in flames. Victims of cancer that was running shamelessly amok. I cringed at the collective "God is good" chant because I was ashamed of such a sunny declaration in a room saturated with so much pain. It felt insensitive to ask people who understood a certain level of grief to give God a shout-out when they probably wanted to yank his credentials.

Another reason I keep a good distance from Job's story is because I have no clue what to do with someone else's loss. Job demands that we just sit with him and be present without solution or consolation, without imparting some big takeaway lesson. His friends find this impossible to pull off, a tendency I can appreciate because I'm the person who makes busyness out of grief. If you were to lose someone you love and you needed a friend to organize some food for the family or pick up people from the airport or make copies of the program for the memorial service, I'm your gal. I can sink myself into a to-do list with the efficiency of a Navy SEAL on virtually no notice, and you will have the nicest post-funeral finger sandwiches you had ever hoped for. (You did hope for that, right?)

Just please don't ask me to sit perfectly still next to you, our fingers laced together in silence as the casket comes down the aisle. Please don't ask me to get down on my hands and knees and help you gather up the fragments of your heart and hold them carefully in my palm like tiny paper birds. I might be able to do that for about thirty seconds, but then I'm gonna start asking around for a glue stick to get busy fixing their wings.

Please don't ask me to simply *be* and to *feel* and not to *do.*

It's here, however, that Job begins to read to his reluctant student between the lines of his great loss. So I lean in a little closer to listen. He begins with the bad news: there is nothing anyone can *do.* Then he starts to reveal things several layers beneath the surface, and I find myself setting aside the weathered and worn "How could a loving God . . . " questions in favor of deeper, even scarier ones. Like the idea that being irreverently honest with God about our sorrow and anger might, in fact, propel us into a deeper place with him that we couldn't have journeyed to otherwise. I've heard people talk about this post-furnace refinement, saying that losing their child brought a depth and beauty to their faith they hadn't known otherwise. It's hard to swallow.

They'll tell you that when they stopped finishing every weeping frenzy with a comment about God's sovereignty . . . when they just allowed their anger to dangle there in the empty silent space between Maker and man, they actually could crawl in closer to his heart. Because honesty is the foundation of intimacy, and they had told God the ugly truth about how they felt about what he had permitted. They realized God could handle it. Actually wanted to handle it.

Could it be, Job asks me, that God actually beckons us into the kind of raw lament that won't be shushed or soothed? Maybe Job tore his shirt into rags because he knew that the best way to beat his chest was to pound actual fist on actual flesh, unhindered by the gathers and folds of the garment between. So that he could confront God with his naked rage, bare-chested like Adam with nothing to hide. Insisting that the Creator stare at his creation, a reminder of the very skin he had wrapped around his own image. Demanding an explanation. Furious tears spilling down wind-burned cheeks and a sunken collarbone, washing over a wrinkled chest where, just below, his heart beat in agony.

These are the kinds of moments we are certain must be rooted in prideful arrogance. Who are we to demand explanations from God? Who are we to rage in full view of the world? Or even worse, the church? How dare we assert that we might have been abandoned?

But what if Job is trying to teach us that God grants us every permission to do just that? Because when our grief has wrung us out like a rag and we are left with no more answers than we had at the start, something inside us breaks wide open. The transformation takes place when we scream the unthinkable at the One who loves us most, only to find not rebuke in response but more bottomless love . . . *that* is what allows us crawl into the crook of his arm and pass out.

So that he might rock us for a while.

A newborn baby's vision is limited to about five inches in front of his face. A newborn's understanding of life is limited to about zero inches in front of her heart. Able to experience pain with no ability to interpret it. And so the Father pulls us in closer and continues rocking after we are exhausted and emptied of our tears.

Awhile back, in the church bulletin, I noticed that there would be a series of Wednesday night services as part of our preparation for the season of Lent. Following each service, we would gather to break bread and, apparently, slurp soup and feast on the nourishment of food and friendship. They needed people to bring soup, and I love to cook. And I love soup. I signed up for a Wednesday night.

And then I forgot about the whole thing.

My schedule that week was insane. I did what I have not done in a long time, which is to severely overcommit to far too many things. All things I loved. I had agreed to do some volunteer work. I had scheduled a few days to write with an artist who was flying all the way to Tulsa in the middle of her tour. I needed to finish writing some songs I had started with a different artist, and I was already significantly behind on my chapter deadlines for this very book. I had several different babysitters lined up for Pepper for way more hours than I was comfortable with. For six nights in a row I went to bed around 2:00 a.m. and set my alarm for 6:00 a.m. It sucked. It was sort of like having a brand-new baby. I just accepted the fact that sleep would not be a part of my life for a time and tried to make peace with my own drool.

As the week began, I literally had every single moment accounted for. No room for changes. Room only for survival.

(Teensy balance issues.)

Then I got the e-mail reminding me that I had volunteered to bring homemade soup to Wednesday night church. In God's goodness, my children were not around to hear the string of colorful adjectives I let fly. I spent at least ten minutes drafting an imaginary reply with creative and believable lies about why I had to withdraw from soup duty. It never occurred to me to actually tell the truth which was, "I'm so sorry. I thought I could. But I just can't."

The voice of guilt was slightly louder than the voice of dishonesty, so I found myself at the grocery store at 10:00 p.m. shopping and then making ninety-two gallons of my famous homemade chicken and rice soup. When I finished scrubbing every last pot and pan that Tuesday night, it was 3:12 a.m. I decided, in my delirium, that I would simply drop the soup off at church, not stay for the service, and then I would drive home, drunk with exhaustion and face-plant on the nearest couch.

Again came the voice of guilt.

*Geez, Nichole. Here's a crazy idea for Lent: How about giving up your big important self for once? Never mind chocolate or french fries or shallow cable TV, why not give up your "I'm-such-a-busy-sacrificial-martyr-I-can-only-drop-off-my-delicious-soup-but-can't-stay-for-church" self? So typical of false piety. Make sure everyone is nourished but very publicly ignore your own hunger.*

*Oh, it's like that?* I answered myself. *FINE. I'll stay for the service. Who needs four hours of sleep when obviously three should be sufficient?*

Let me add here that, at the time, our pastor had been walking us through the importance of praying prayers of lament. In fact, he called it an art. The art of lament. He introduced us to a bunch of scripture centered around mourning. Rooted in anger. Offering no emotional payoff or relief, just raw honesty before God about our loss and the appalling notion that he would leave us out there on the high hill of pain and then stay hidden as we call out for him.

*How long, Lord? Will you hide from me forever?* cries the psalmist.

*Why do you hide your face and consider me your enemy?* moans Job.

My God, why have you forsaken me? begs his own Son.

The next night, I dropped my soup off in the fellowship hall, my daughter in the nursery, and snuck into the back row of the church, plopping down in between Duty and his first cousin, Obligation. Hundreds of candles lit the small sanctuary. Perfect for a discreet nap. Subtle and beautiful music hung as a distant backdrop for worship. Not many were singing. Hands were held in laps. There was a distinct unnamed heaviness in the room. To my dismay, I realized I had crashed the lament service our pastor had warned us about. People had come to grieve while I was merely there to make an appearance.

Pastor Ed said a few words about what we could expect. A few thoughts on how the Lord was not afraid of the grief that lurked in our hearts. A few more thoughts on what it might cost us *not* to acknowledge grief but to trade vulnerability in favor of the quick "God is good" moment. And what we lose in that transaction.

With great affection for the candlelight, I reluctantly settled in. Then he asked everyone to please come forward to the front of the church and find a comfortable place to kneel on the floor during the service.

Oh. So this is gonna be like a participatory thing, then.

We each found a spot on the floor, and immediately something shifted in me. Something physical. The small move from chair to floor was a substantial one for the posture of my heart. The ground felt like the proper place for sitting with grief. Except that I didn't have any. Still, I was glad for everyone else, and I thought that sitting close to those who were grieving might help me pray for them more earnestly. Slowly, I was becoming invested in this experience.

For the next thirty minutes our hearts were led to lament specific needs around the world. We sat encircled by candles, awkwardly close to other knees and elbows, and watched as different photographs were projected up on the screen. Like a photo of a hungry child. Then someone would read a prayer, asking essentially, "Why God? Why would you let children go hungry in a world where there is such abundance? How could you allow people to remain in positions of power who do nothing except take more? Do you not see and hear the cries of the mothers who have nothing to give their children? Where are you?" Then we would sit in silence and just let the sorrow hang there.

As the prayer went on, I felt my throat tighten. I saw the well-fed faces of my own children in my mind and was suddenly appalled that any mother had to hold a starving child. Appalled and angry, I felt the tears beginning to fall.

We prayed a similar prayer of lament beneath a photograph of a newborn's tiny foot, and we cried out for all the lives lost to terminated pregnancies. We cried for their mothers too, and for whatever financial or social situation was so dire they felt they had to make this choice. We lamented the horrors of modern-day slavery around the world. Little-boy soldiers. Little-girl prostitutes. We offered up our indignation and sorrow, and each time I bristled at how open-ended we left things. Our laments were never resolved with a promise or an assurance or a statement about God's goodness.

Then, when we had grieved as a group for things that broke our collective heart, Ed opened up some time for personal lament. I assumed this meant we would spend a few moments in quiet reflective prayer, taking our own small sorrows before God. Instead, he asked us to name our grief out loud. To find Job's voice within us and call out to God, or maybe just call God out, rattling our well-kept cages and setting sorrow free. He said it would probably be uncomfortable for us but not for God.

I am always struck by how different cultures grieve. The Western world is so private and reserved. Buttoned up behind closed doors. Dabbing our dignified tears with folded tissues. The images in different corners of the world of people wailing in the streets at the news of tragedy make me uncomfortable. Rocking and weeping and moaning. A cacophony of anguish so loud and demonstrative, I have to look away or change the channel. I feel ashamed to bear witness to something so raw and personal. Yet no doubt, their way is far healthier.

For this reason, I had a bad (and hopeful) feeling no one was going to speak up.

But it was almost as if once permission had been granted, the floodgates opened wide, and people started lining up with their broken hearts. Immediately, a woman stood, bawling, almost yelling at God for the devastating choice her friend had made to abort her baby.

"How could you let this happen?" she cried. "My friend grew up knowing you. She loves you! And now I will never know this baby. My own babies will never run and play with that beautiful child!" She was choking on small sobs. "Whyyy, God?"

People began to cry quietly with her. Openly.

Ed invited us to say together with the psalmist, "How long, O Lord? How long?"

Another voice, loud and shaky: "Why is it taking so long to adopt this child? Four and a half years? I'm so angry at you. There are so many children who need families. I don't understand what you're doing! Did you forget about us??"

We wept with her. For her empty arms. For a motherless child somewhere.

And then we asked quietly together, "How long, Lord?"

"Why won't you heal our baby?" came a shattered voice from the back. "Why does he have to endure these horrible seizures? He's never done anything to anyone. He's a BABY! You could stop this if you wanted to. Why won't you?"

*How long, Lord?*

The lamenting went on and on. I looked up through my tears for a moment and saw a room full of grown men and women, shirts and ties from the office, skinny jeans, yoga pants, ball caps. Faces in their hands, kneeling in ash heaps. Trying to work through their own aching and fury. Trying to hand their tiny paper birds to the only One who could give them wings again, although who knows how or when or if he even would.

A few times, quick disclaimers would follow a person's loud lament, almost like a frightened apology.

" . . . and still Lord, we know you are able to work all things together for your good . . ."

Then Ed would gently pause and remind us not to feel pressure to wrap up our sorrow in bright-colored ribbons. God doesn't need to be let off the hook. Ed would help us try again to simply name our sorrows and nothing else.

I knew there were many kneeling there who, like me, were nursing their sorrow privately. Who, like me, could not find the courage to stand and speak their grief out loud. I hoped someone could hear me yelling on the inside, *God!!! Why?? Why would you allow my marriage to implode like this?? Why would you let so much scar tissue grow over my heart that I can no longer even feel the wound? Where are you? I've spent years pointing fearful people to you. Assuring them you're not a leaver. Did you leave?? Say something!!"*

*How long, O Lord?*

I realized, after a time, that I had been sitting, hugging wet knees to my chest, rocking back and forth. Wanting to be rocked. But rocking myself. Wanting to be held. But holding myself.

Pepper and I drove home in near silence, which was strange for my chatty girl. I was weary and done in. Staring off, not noticing when red lights turned green. It had been years since I had turned inward to that degree, to face my sadness and my loneliness. I had kept myself good and busy for too long. Made a lot of soup. While God waited.

No answers came. I hollered into an abyss, and nobody hollered back.

But as my head hit the pillow, I felt the smallest flash of understanding of why we call it a *sacrifice* of praise. It *is* sacrificial. It costs a lot to still worship the One who allows the wound. It costs a lot to bless the One who both fills our cups and lets them spill. Who gives, and then without explanation, takes away.

Walter Brueggemann wrote in his book *The Prophetic Imagination*, "Weeping must be real because endings are real" and "that weeping permits newness."[1] Job knew, perhaps more than anyone, what the sky looks like after a storm. When the torrents of rain have cleaned the dust from the air, your pain is still present, but you can see it more clearly. You can see everything more clearly. You notice that you are not alone in your sorrow. God weeps too, for you and with you. And he's making room on his lap to rock you, when you're ready. And still love you, if you're not.

◎

*As for me, I know that my Redeemer lives, and at the last He
will take His stand on the earth. Even after my skin is destroyed,
Yet from my flesh I shall see God. (Job 19:25–26 NASB)*

# broken praise
## job
Lyrics from *Music Inspired by The Story*

If one more person takes my hand
And tries to say they understand,
Tells me there's a bigger plan that I'm not meant to see.
If one more person dares suggest
That I held something unconfessed,
Tries to make the dots connect from righteousness to
easy street . . .

Well I, I won't deny that I've relied on some assumptions.
A man's honest life entitles him to something,
But who am I to make demands of the God of Abraham?
And who are you that you would choose to answer me
with mercy new?
How many more will wander past
To find me here among the ashes?
Will you hold me? Will you stay
So I can raise this broken praise to you?

Who else will see my suffering
As one more opportunity
To educate; to help me see all my flawed theology?

If one more well-intentioned friend tries to tie up
    my loose ends
Hoping to, with rug and broom, sweep awkward
    moments from the room . . .
But I, I can't forget that I have begged just like
    a madman
For my chance to die and never have to face
    the morning.

But you were the One who filled my cup
And you were the One who let it spill.
So blessed be your holy name if you never fill it
    up again.
If this is where my story ends, just give me one more
    breath to say hallelujah.

*mary*

# things to write in wet cement

I WAS TELLING my therapist recently about my terminal case of people pleasing and how easily paralyzed I am by the faintest whiff of disapproval. It's just so absurd. But so very real. Even the slightest smug, judgmental glance from Martha across the restaurant (an immaculate woman who is *not* digging her toddler's mac and cheese out of her bra) can send me into a tailspin, resulting in one of two scenarios: (A) I will limp behind her all the way to her Lexus, apologizing for being such a frayed mother with misbehaving children and a woefully inadequate bra, or (B) I will quietly explain to my kids, through a steeled jaw, that we do not care about that mean lady. She is not a Christian. And the first one to make a voodoo doll out of french fries in her likeness gets a sucker. Then I will excuse myself to retrieve the promised sucker and let the air out of her tires. I am not going to be diminished by a woman wearing seven-inch eyelashes and chewing Prada gum.

In these moments, my best friends across the table are well rehearsed in lovingly mouthing *Let. It. Go.*

Excuse me? A total stranger has frowned at me with slight disapproval? Who lets it go, I ask you??

Oh. *You* do.

I swear to you, I don't know how this came to be. Both of my parents raised me to rise above petty insecurities that might tether my self-esteem to someone else's opinion. To follow instinct and not crowds. To shrug off criticism and condescension and pay attention instead to who I know I am and, more importantly, who God says I am.

I vaguely remember being that person once.

But I felt something dramatically shift in my self-esteem when I became a recording artist. Before that, I was a career student, during which and certainly after which I was a career waitress. I felt pretty okay about being a waitress because I was good at it, and everyone agreed on that point. I have a black belt in multitasking and could take simultaneous orders for seven tables, never write a single thing down, bring out the hot food in a timely manner, and suggest an appropriate wine that would complement the linguini. When my customers felt I had served them well, they rewarded me with a generous gratuity. The end.

Nobody sped home to blog about my performance with the parmesan grater. I never tweeted a favorite passage of Scripture that really inspired my shift. Nobody had to slap a marketing sticker on the front of my apron to sell me to the customer, and I did not spend two hours in hair and makeup before Meatball Monday.

Then one Saturday night in Santa Monica, I got my shift covered so I could enter a songwriting competition with a song I wrote that was around sixteen minutes long. The judges let me win so that the song might mercifully end, and less than a year later I was hauling all my possessions to Nashville in my '96 Chevy Cavalier to work on my first solo project. Collaborating and recording music was a high like none other I had known. I didn't think I could ever be happier or more fulfilled.

But once I finished writing and dreaming and recording, I was suddenly noshing on a steady twenty-four-hour-a-day diet of someone else's opinion of my music and my life. I was terrified about what was being spoken, written, critiqued, and picked apart as I slept naively through the night. I could hardly function from the paranoia. I was frantic for everyone, from the radio station to the mail room, to love and adore my fledgling new music, and that just wasn't statistically possible.

Now that I have the embarrassing gift of perspective and an ounce more maturity, I can easily roll my eyes about this painful chapter. I've heard the claims that artistic people are a wee more insecure than the rest of the humans on our planet. I have to agree. I would add self-absorbed.

I think when you choose to live your life and your art publicly, you also unknowingly plant the small, inevitable seed of narcissism in the garden of your heart. Whether it grows into the kind of thick and impenetrable jungle that's begging for a machete or simply sprouts up as the occasional weed that needs a good tug is a matter of what your sprinkler system looks like.

In response to my obsession with other people's opinion about my life, my therapist shared with me that the average amount of time a person spends thinking about another person is around eight seconds at a time before he or she starts thinking me-related thoughts again. That's it. Just eight seconds. Even if it's your mom. Or your spouse. Or the news about your pastor's wife's cancer diagnosis. It's not that we are incapable of empathy, but eight seconds is about all our self-absorbed leachy little human souls can manage before we begin sucking on our own skin again, trying to get drunk on ourselves.

In other words, Nichole, nobody thinks about you that much, sweetie pie.

I glanced up at him from my text.

I'm sorry, I sniffed, were you saying something?

Was it about me?

My preoccupation with self and the approval of others began at an early age. Some of those memories are still clear enough to snorkel in.

I attended a small Christian school, and in the fifth grade my teacher wrote my name on the upper-left corner of the chalkboard, the section reserved for criminals, ne'er-do-wells, and kids who played with matches. It was the first and only time this happened. I was probably talking out of turn or braiding my friend's hair when I should have been locating the capital of Nebraska on a map. No biggie, it was a gentle warning in chalk. He didn't cane me on the knee pits. Besides, the chalkboard ordeal happened to lots of the other kids all day long.

Just . . . not to me.

I still remember that devastating, bottomless feeling of failure. I looked straight down at the US map on my desk while large lakes of tears pooled inside my pink glasses, observing, in my distress, that Nebraska suddenly had a coast. With such a public failure, word would inevitably spread before recess, which meant I had exactly two hours to find a quarter for the pay phone and re-enroll in a different school. It was over. How did these people expect me to carry this reputation into the sixth grade? Why didn't I just go ahead and start handing out cigarettes after lunch?

Years later, when I was sixteen, I called my mom twenty minutes before my curfew. I was at a friend's house, and it had begun really storming outside. The car I drove that summer was a Jeep Renegade with the hard top off—because that is the law, if you own a Jeep during a Colorado summer. The open air is far too glorious to legalize the use of windows. The weather guy was saying that the rain would continue for several hours, and I told my groggy mom on the phone that I didn't really want to drive home in that open-air Jeep during a storm; I wanted to sleep on my friend's couch instead. She agreed, thanked me for calling, and said she expected to see me first thing tomorrow.

When I strolled in the next morning with my 7-Eleven donut, right away I knew something was horribly wrong. Both my parents looked like they had crawled out of a Tim Burton movie, all crazy limbs with wiry hair and black beady eyes darting around like roaches. Tossing the phone to each other. Pacing the floor. Pressed up against windows. Rubbing their temples with their roachy fingers. Trying to Lamaze breathe.

I stood there for a few seconds eating my donut, observing this madness with a growing unease, until I said in the smallest voice possible, "Hello? Everything okay?"

Oh.

It was so very *not* okay.

My mom, who could never even really pull off a decent spanking when I was little, suddenly lunged at me with some insane pile-driver move followed by an epic sobbing attempt to kiss my face off. My dad initially just glared across the kitchen like, *Well, how nice of you to join us, young lady, and how are things going down at the METH LAB this fine morning?* Then he moved in with bone-crushing hugs while my mom resumed the punching/kissing bit.

It took us a very short time to figure out that Mom had answered the phone in a deep sleep the night before and had no memory of our conversation. No memory of the rain. The friend's couch. The responsible daughter who called before curfew. Actually this came as no real shock to anyone because the woman could sleep through the Pasadena Rose Parade. On a float. My parents had been on the phone since daylight trying to locate me, calling hospitals and morgues, well-known cult compounds, and anyone they'd ever met, including those they might have chatted with on a plane for five minutes. I barely beat the sheriff to my house.

Within a few minutes of solving the mystery, they collapsed into the exhausted laughter of fresh relief while my mom kept doing the "I coulda had a V8" smack on her forehead. Such a silly goose!

Hey, it happens, chuckled my understanding dad. What a dang hoot!

I was livid.

LI. VID.

I didn't speak to Mom for hours and hours. Maybe days.

I was sure that all of Douglas County was under the (albeit brief) impression that I was one of those sketchy teenagers, out until dawn with my smudgy black eyeliner, sitting in a mall parking lot with public school kids listening to Depeche Mode. And doing God knows what else. All the parents, all the teachers, the ER nurses, and morticians thought that I was THAT kid. And I was anything *but* that kid. (I was that kid much later.) My entire reputation had been dragged through the gutter because my own mother was too sleepy to remember how perfect and responsible I was.

With my hypersensitivity to the opinions of others, and my determination to maintain a certain image among those who know me, might know me, used to know me, or by chance happened to pass me once on the sidewalk, it's no surprise that I have a particular admiration for Mary, the mother of Jesus, and an appreciation for what it must have cost her teenage heart to bear the weight of the whispers.

We think of Mary with the greatest respect—when we bother to think of her. Usually that happens at Christmas (and if we are honest, usually *only* at Christmas, unless maybe we're Catholic). We start reflecting in earnest about the girl who gave us Jesus. Like so many of the most beloved characters in Scripture, she has become spectacularly simplified. It's an inescapable part of our Christian culture. Ask a child what color Elmo is, and he will say red. Ask him about the color of Mary's robe in the manger scene, and he will say blue. Church nativity plays and artists' renderings for years have given us not just Mary's wardrobe but her posture as well. Kneeling. Hovering. Glowing. Beaming. Adoring.

But let's get real. This is childbirth, folks. Where is the tsunami of sweat? The fresh claw marks on Joseph's arm? And I have yet to see an artist depict what the straw beneath Mary would really have looked like.

I'm not going to waste valuable ink trying to paint a more realistic birthing picture. You've heard the stories. If you aren't a mom, ask one. Then watch for this universal response. She will shudder a little and then exhale sharply through pursed lips and mutter something like, "Totally worth it . . . totally, totally worth it."

I was flooded with Mary thoughts as I saw my neighbors' teenage daughter the other day. She is a sweetheart, totally trustworthy, and a great baby- and housesitter. Watching through the window as she walked her little dog, I tried to imagine what it would be like to be about her age, going about your business, housesitting for a neighbor one minute, and nine months later find yourself entrenched in fresh animal manure, bearing down in labor and slicing the darkness with a scream too primal for filmmakers to ever really replicate convincingly.

The birth alone is enough reason to honor Mary.

Her emotional journey is another.

Apart from the arduous trek to Bethlehem, some other familiar themes present themselves in her story. Her fierce obedience, her courage and raw sacrifice, for starters. Her circumstance was so unthinkable. So unfair, from my perspective. From her Magnificat in the gospel of Luke, we know that her soul magnified the Lord and that her spirit rejoiced when she learned of her role in God's gripping love letter to the world. At some point she understood (at least in part) the priceless honor bestowed upon her.

It just makes me wonder when, in her teenage heart, she reconciled that same honor with all the dishonor she would endure. I wonder if before acceptance, before resolve and joy, she felt even a little dread. I wonder if she cared about the whispers.

I wonder if she ever wished she hadn't been picked.

Like that moment when you're lined up in gym class. Speaking for myself, I do my best to block these memories.

I am the least athletic person you'll ever meet. Walking upright is a daily miracle that I celebrate. I was equally uncoordinated as a child and teen. This is a matter for another time, but why do gym teachers make such a colossal event out of singling out nonathletes? I don't remember my choir teacher saying, "Okay, folks! Everyone who's an awesome singer, line up over here, and we'll call you the captains. Then you may select your teammates from the devastating options of nonsingers in this other line, a virtual wasteland of tone deafness. Good luck, everybody! And remember, we're all winners!"

This absolutely did not happen in choir class. Not in algebra either, I noticed. It was just another special perk of PE.

I knew in any lineup for a kickball game, it was all over for me. I was the least likely to do anything respectable on a gym floor, except possibly clean it. I prayed fervently for the Rapture every single time. There is nothing worse than being singled out and asked to display your insecurities and weaknesses for all. Time and time again, the nonathletes' anthem rises up from the gangliest of us. *Dontpickme. Dontpickme. Dontpickme.*

That day when Mary found herself shaking in front of the towering, fearsome angel and finally understood the reason for his visit, I wonder if the first echoes of that anthem might have been stuck in her throat like a frantic internal whisper.

*Dontpickme. Dontpickme. Dontpickme.*

I wonder when exactly she came to terms with what it would cost her emotionally and socially. No surprise, that's the part of Mary's story that really levels me. I would honestly rather give birth in a barn, without an epidural, than have to tell people that God got me pregnant and face their ridicule day after humiliating day. To have to watch my parents' faces, torn between the desperate need to believe me and everything that common sense is asking of them instead. To shuffle around the streets with a growing belly and the very lonely knowledge that it's the Messiah who's kicking my ribs. Those are situations my pride would just never allow. I would have to scream, instead, from every thatched roof, "JUST YOU WAIT, SUCKERS!!! JUST YOU WAIT!!!"

This would be why Gabriel might, in great haste, lose my address.

It's also why, for me, the heart of Mary's story is her astonishing humility. Humility as both an initial response and an ongoing choice. That's a new idea for me. I think of humility as something you have or do not. Like DNA, camping out on a chromosome. Humility is like a dimple or a widow's peak. It doesn't respond to effort. It just is.

I don't think about people *choosing* humility. I have trouble putting myself in Mary's sandals as she woke up every morning, splashed water on her face, and opened the door to a community snickering about her "situation," and then *choosing* humility. Her decision to diminish herself enough to make room for Jesus makes me want to cry.

My teenage memories are too fresh perhaps. Here's a recap. Me: the sun. You: orbiting.

I wonder if she had any normal teen moments in the face of all this. I can't help but think she may have wept some bitter tears in her mother's lap despite how her soul magnified the Lord. I think maybe her mother wept a little too over all the normal and wonderful moments they would never know together. The wedding. The children. The traditions and memories. The stuff of moms and daughters. Instead she watched her baby, heavy with another, climb on a mule and head into the darkness toward an unknown future. A future where mothers don't hold the hands of daughters in labor. Or rock their grandsons. The death of even a routine dream is still a death.

Perhaps Mary, having understood the magnitude of being hand-chosen by God, was still looking over her shoulder once or twice on the way out of town . . . watching her simple hopes dissolve as the night swallowed her. Maybe her head was able to process the intellectual knowledge of God's amazing favor, but surely it took awhile for her heart to catch up. But that's okay, isn't it? To feel reluctant in the face of the extraordinary dreams of God because we're having a little trouble prying our fingers off our own dreams for the weekend? I live there.

Like everyone else, I think of Mary at Christmas. But my images of her aren't always of her trembling before the angel on her bedroom floor. Or in a stable, backlit with candles while pressing her beautiful baby to her breast.

I picture her, instead, standing alone at night, in the middle of a construction site. Almost alone, that is.

I watch her pick up a small stick in the street, step over the warning cones and caution tape and kneel down at the foundation of what will one day be a beautiful chapel. She knows she will never see its walls or its stained glass. She will never sit in its pews or kneel at its altar. She won't ever experience firsthand the tears of worship and the joy the world will offer the baby inside her. Somehow she knows this. But for a moment in history, she kneels at the foundation of it all, with the hope of the world sitting on her bony shoulders, the question and crisis of all mankind begging for an answer.

I watch her find a fresh square of wet cement and then freeze for just a moment, hovering over it. For more than eight seconds. She closes her eyes and breathes in the night air. Then, with a fresh and trembling courage and the small stroke of a twig, I watch her scrawl the word *yes.*

The yes that will be etched into the foundation of the world for all time.

The yes the angels breathlessly awaited.

The kind of yes that is deaf to opinion or gossip or petty concern about reputation.

A yes that is immune to self.

A yes that isn't even concerned with the details of the question . . . because God is the asker.

She turns and wraps her shawl around herself against the wind. It's blue. And she continues into the dark alone. Almost alone, that is. And then I hear her whisper.

*Totally worth it.*
*Totally, totally worth it.*

*"I am the Lord's servant," Mary answered. "May it be to me as you have said." Then the angel left her. (Luke 1:38 NIV1984)*

# be born in me
## *mary*
### Lyrics from *Music Inspired by The Story*

Everything inside me cries for order,
Everything inside me wants to hide.
Is this shadow an angel or a warrior?
If God is pleased with me, why am I so terrified?

Someone tell me I am only dreaming,
Somehow help me see with heaven's eyes.
And before my head agrees, my heart is on its knees,
Holy is he. Blessed am I.

Be born in me, be born in me.
Trembling heart, somehow I believe that you
    chose me.
I'll hold you in the beginning,
You will hold me in the end.
Every moment in the middle, make my heart your
    Bethlehem.

Be born in me.
All this time we've waited for the promise,
All this time you've waited for my arms.
Did you wrap yourself inside the unexpected
So we might know that Love would go that far?

I am not brave,
I'll never be;
The only thing my heart can offer is a vacancy.
I'm just a girl,
Nothing more,
But I am willing.
I am yours.

*jesus*
# glitter cows

IF YOU WANT to know what something's really worth, what its *true* value is, don't bother asking the person who is either selling it or trying to buy it. Don't ask the people who determine value by taking perfectly innocent numbers and then . . . what's the expression? . . . crunching them. (And why must the numbers be so violently crunched? demands the sensitive writer. I don't take words and *bludgeon* them . . . )

By true worth, I'm not talking about the value of a gold bracelet or how much your car has depreciated since you drove it off the lot three years ago. Those kinds of buyers and sellers calculate and appraise all day long. For fun. Don't ask them.

Ask the person who cares about the item most. Ask the person who cares about it too much, maybe. To the point of irrational absurdity. The kind of caring that makes other people shake their heads and look the other way as you sneak something out of your box of "Garage Sale Items" and back into your closet for the ninth time, under cover of darkness, perhaps.

Just try and put a price tag on your grandfather's dusty old trumpet. Or a sentimental piece of art. These things can never really be properly evaluated because hearts don't speak the jargon of appraisal.

Lost-kitty posters are the worst. Especially when there's a five-hundred-dollar reward beneath the face of some grumpy old calico that was probably a freebie rescue kitten from a shelter thirteen years ago. The reward money tells you everything you need to know. Baseball card collections get sold. Piggy banks get smashed to raise money for kitty's reward. Empty arms know what kitty is worth.

Or take art, for example. If you really want to understand the value of a piece of art, don't consult an art dealer, busy inflating his stratospheric profit margins. Stand quietly in a museum facing a single piece with someone who has a bone-deep appreciation for every small subtlety. Every shaft of light or hint of movement. You will marvel at all that is held sacred by the art lover—and totally lost on you. If you're open to seeing what she sees, you might start to value it differently. That's what I've heard anyway.

My friend Luci is an art connoisseur. She's studied art formally, she knows it well, and she inhales and exhales art's history, nuance, and emotion. She is the consummate artist. (Just between us, I've noticed that artists are not overly enthusiastic about being described as *artsy*. The word screams pipe cleaners and hot glue guns. We would never call you *sciencey*. Or *doctorish*.)

One time Luci drew me a map to her house, and I almost framed it. The woman could make a grocery list with a paper towel and Sharpie, and all the art majors in Florence would gnash their teeth. Luci's home is homage to diverse and beautiful pieces that resonate deep within her, each with a meaningful story. And I've noticed she is actually even more beautiful herself in their presence.

I'm told there is no one better to stroll with through an art museum than Luci. I've wanted to but never have. I'm paranoid that I would get too restless and ADD-ish and find myself interrogating the security guards about *How could there not be a snack bar?* and would inevitably be a general embarrassment to all. Being still is not my strength. Quiet is my strength, but it must be a productive quiet, like reading or writing. Not art museum quiet, like staring.

Luci was among the dear friends I traveled with on that recent trip to Guatemala. We had a day off in La Antigua, and Luci, of course, made time to stroll through a few local art museums. *My chance!* I thought.

But then I zip-lined through a jungle instead.

It's all in what you value. I bow out of the museum tour, but I absolutely have the stillness capacity to sit through a three-hour symphony performance without the slightest eyelash tremor. Because music transfixes me. Music and I "get" each other intimately. We finish each other's sentences. We blush shamelessly across crowded rooms. I understand its worth because, to me, it's worth everything. I know why musicians played those stringed instruments on the *Titanic*'s deck as the black sea swallowed that beautiful beast, one gilded gold inch at a time. It pierces my heart when my friend Jason, who battles a minor stutter in speech, can sing with effortless grace, leaving me in tears. I understand why my grandfather can no longer remember faces or names, including my own, but can recall every last lyric to "My Funny Valentine" and a hundred other songs buried in his memory's catacombs. The emotional powers of the arts defy rational explanation. Crunch all the numbers you like, some things can't be appraised.

And forget museums and galleries for a second. Just stand with a grandma in front of a refrigerator with hand-drawn pictures fixed to it. Watch the way she traces every scribble and smudged drawing. Watch how she marvels at the primitive mess of glue and glitter. Listen to her go on and on (and on), gushing about how nobody draws better cows than her grandchild. Nobody. I mean, this kid has a serious future in glitter cows. You get the impression Grandma would trip a couple of kindergartners on the sidewalk if they dared disagree.

No one else sees what Grandma sees, probably not even Mom (perhaps because Mom spends her life wiping glitter off the dog's rear parts). Grandma would tackle any sucker who tried to remove even a single masterpiece from its proper place on her fridge. She alone knows that artwork's value.

I may not be an art connoisseur, but I know what I like (even if I don't know why). I own several framed prints from Matisse's Blue Nudes series. I love Matisse, especially this series. It's simple and playful. Clean lines. Almost juvenile, and my favorite shade of blue ever. I actually saw one of the originals in Paris years ago and was struck by how small it seemed—because I am so accustomed to my giant replica from POSTERZ R US. (Thank you, America.)

This series was one of Matisse's last contributions before his death. In fact, he died before the series could be published. He had grown incredibly weak, confined to either wheelchair or bed as he was being kicked around by stomach cancer. He could no longer stand or bend and linger over a painting. Nor could he step back against the far wall in his studio to gain perspective mid-process. His craft was confined to whatever small movements he could manage while sitting or lying down. So he traded in his beloved paints and grabbed a pair of scissors. He painstakingly cut out each shape for the Blue Nudes and then hand painted them before directing his assistants how to carefully arrange them on the canvas. Imagine how maddening this must have been for an artist of his caliber, once so capable and independent.

"No, no, Anton, I said a little to the left. *Left! LEEEEFT!!!*" And then he would swear at poor Anton like a drunken sailor—which, being French and all, would still just sound like a loud poem.

He couldn't stop creating. His limitations simply forced him to adapt and change his medium and approach.

When I heard this story for the first time, I teared up. I try to imagine having my fingers amputated, well into my eighth decade, ending my love affair with the piano and lining the dim halls of my memory with longing for what could be no more. And I wonder, would I just roll over and wait for death? Or would I adapt? Blaze a new trail. Try to forget the way a diminished seventh chord feels beneath my fingers before it resolves? Would I take up whistling? Tap dance?

To someone who doesn't know the history of Matisse's process and genius, the Blue Nudes look like someone did a better than average job with a pair of a scissors and a stack of blue origami paper. I confirmed this a few weeks ago when I was sitting at my table having coffee with sweet Carie, my dear older friend from India who regularly plows through the din of my dirty house until it shines. She pointed at the largest of the Blue Nudes on the wall and asked earnestly, "Deed you paint dat?"

Because and only because Carie really loves me (she said so), if I had said yes, she would have marveled at my talent and gone on and on about my keen understanding of form and space. There would have been much oohing and aahing.

But of course I laughed and said no. No, I did not. Henri Matisse did that.

Hmm, she shrugged, not so impressed.

(Glitter cows.)

Those are the thoughts that usurp my own when I consider the Creator's work and the way he and I value it. Sometimes when I am overcome with emotion at something beautiful I have read or seen or touched, I realize (as if I hadn't before) that it was God who had the idea first. That God, with careful intention, added every gauzy layer of petals to a white peony. It wasn't something that just happened in my garden one morning.

The first several chapters of Genesis will always be, for me, much more about beauty than it will ever be about science. I know I should feel compelled to jump into the evolution debate and be clear about which side of the fence my faith dictates I land on. It's not that I don't care. I just don't have the energy to try and understand something that can't be understood by the three-pound lump of gray matter tucked beneath my skull. At my core, I know this: God is God. All that lives and breathes flows from him in both original and ongoing states.

The color of a robin's eggs, the shape of a jalapeño pepper, the smell of Lake Michigan in July—it's all evidence of a profoundly creative God. Let someone else argue about carbon dating. (Numbers. Numbers. Crunch. Crunch.) You'll find me planting marigolds, because that's where I find him.

If then, God, the Artist, took a universe-sized canvas and stood, brush in hand, giddy with anticipation, before taking that first sweeping stroke across it . . . how much more tragic it must have been for Jesus to find his Father's masterpiece sticking out of a filthy Dumpster. Trampled and tossed. Smeared with the stench of a selfish people who care nothing for the Artist or the art because they care nothing for themselves. They don't know they are his pièce de résistance.

Amazingly, this is where Jesus sets up shop for his short

stay on our broken planet. Next to the Dumpster. Every day he rolls up his sleeves, lurches over the side, and lowers himself into the muck so he can begin recovering and restoring the remains of his Father's original perfect work. Lo and behold, beneath the strata of filth and decay, he finds people actually living and sleeping in there too.

This will never do.

I majored in psychology (and just about everything else at some point) and will always be deeply interested in human behavior and why folks do what they do. I was not cut out for a career in psychology but still found a way to be around a bunch of head cases, among whom I am chief. My life as a musician affords me this.

I'm fascinated by how the world of counseling and therapy has grown and adapted to meet the needs of hurting people everywhere. I'm a big fan of therapy. Spent a lot of time on a lot of couches, blowing my nose. I am so thankful to have learned so much *about* myself that I never could have muddled through *by* myself. Well, mostly thankful.

But today the field has changed from just couches and Kleenex.

Brutally abused women are caring for gentle horses and learning how to feel safe again, one apple, one muzzle at a time. Reclaiming trust.

Returning combat soldiers suffering from PTSD are sitting with therapy dogs. Speaking a tiny bit more each day about the horrors they've seen as an unconditional ball of furry love wags its tail patiently and never asks questions. Healing begins.

Children, tormented by ongoing memories of what Hurricane Katrina etched into their small psyches as the water rose around their chests, are still drawing. Drawing a path into the pain because it is too hard to tell someone about sitting on a roof for days with your dead uncle.

If all of this horse/canine/crayon therapy sounds like hocus-pocus, weirdo nonsense to you, I'm thinking you may not have watched as your friends were blown up in a military Humvee or your family drowned. (But thanks for weighing in.)

I like to think of Jesus as an art therapist. Not in a crisp clean classroom but there in the back alley by the Dumpster. I imagine him coaxing people out of the shadows. Pulling back their filthy blankets. Building a fire to warm their hands.

Peter? . . . What happened? Why are you living like this? When did you last bathe? Oh friend, I'm so sorry to find you here. Tell me your story, Peter.

A shaky voice after some silence says, "I can't . . . I . . . I can't talk about it."

All right. That's okay, friend. Tear off some of that cardboard over there. I brought a little paint. You don't have to use words. Choose colors that help. Paint a picture that tells me.

Wait . . . Matthew? Is that you? Come over here a minute. How did it get this bad, buddy? You look like you haven't slept for weeks. It's okay. We're gonna sort this out. Start talking. Tell me your story.

Small sobs. "I don't know where to start."

Don't worry. When you're ready, I want you take this paint and show me what your heart looks like. I think I can take it from there. Yes, of course you can just use your fingers if you can't hold the brush.

Judas. *Judas!* Don't act like you didn't hear me. Come here. No? Fine, I'm coming in. Yes, I'm getting *in* the Dumpster with you. No, I will not just leave you alone. What do I want? Well, a hug for starters. Thank you. Now take this can of spray paint over to that wall there and paint me a picture of why things hurt so bad. Then we can talk about it. I want to know your story.

More people gather. More broken, drunk, filthy people start slinking out of the shadowy corners and limping toward Jesus. No one is able to speak eloquently about his or her shattered life. Few speak at all. Women come cautiously with children peeking out from behind their legs. Nobody is looking for lectures or lessons. Not looking for sermons about poor choices and the consequences of sin. Not aching for some angry reprimand masquerading as tough love. Nobody here has been really jonesing for an accountability partner. Just looking for a new canvas and some paint. And a Savior who will stand over his or her shoulder and whisper questions and encouragement, the way a parent stands over a child.

Tell me why you chose the color red for that. What do those boxes mean? Who is the person with no eyes? I like how the sun is sneaking up over those dark hills. Tell me more of your story . . .

Time and again in the life of Jesus, we watch him leave a trail of beauty in the most unbeautiful places and people. When a woman at a well confesses her shame, he hands her a new easel and tells her to toss all that cheap art that litters her walls at home. When a tax collector is exposed for his shady business dealings, Jesus invites himself to dinner and brings along some watercolors. Together they will hang something on the wall that Zacchaeus can be proud of, remembering the moment he was given a clean canvas. No one could encounter Jesus and be unchanged. No one who asked for paint was ever denied. Each one is an artist by birth. Made in the image of an Artist who has no trouble recognizing his own reflection.

The miracle of the love of Jesus is that it does not require that we even understand why or how we arrived at the Dumpster in such a broken condition. He does not require personality inventories or twelve steps of anything. Even if we are unable to identify our wound, he just shows up . . . as the tourniquet. For the addict, he is Day 1 of sobriety. And Day 1,001. For the abused, he is a hotline. For the depressed, he is the two-inch crack in the heavy drapes where the sunlight spills in. For the thief, he becomes the Hope Diamond. For the indifferent and apathetic, he is a hunger strike. For the shamed and exposed, he is a bathrobe from a five-star hotel. For the smug and self-righteous, he is the homeless guy standing with a sign at the exit ramp.

When Jesus showed up at the Dumpster, his Father got to create again too. Not for seven days but for thirty-three years. He got to say Let There Be Light once more. And then, once more, he could say, It Is Good. Both creation accounts spoke immediate light into darkness. Both cared about small sparrows and lilies. Both stood in the face of sin and despair.

But then God said from the garden, You are finished. You cannot stay.

And his Son said from a cross, *It* is finished. Please don't leave.

Both spoke truth.

After a while, when all the pain has been poured out onto canvas, when all the tears have mingled enough with the paint, when people have had something to eat and cleaned themselves up a bit, Jesus asks everyone to gather their paintings and bring them over to the Dumpster. He knows their stories now. He has seen the images of anguish, the dark silhouettes splattered on white backdrops. Some with hopeful flecks of color, some only in brown and gray, the weary soul's sepia.

He invites them to toss each painting into the Dumpster. And then to walk away, telling a new story about themselves. To buy an easel and a smock and practice painting that new story every day.

Judas looks nervous. His pain has been sprayed, more permanently, like graffiti onto a wall. It won't fit in the Dumpster. Jesus coaxes him to toss the can of spray paint in anyway. He reminds them all of their beauty. Their value. Their true worth as his brothers and sisters, sons and daughters. He reminds them they are not a wound. They are marigolds. Sunsets. Ice-blue glaciers. Everything beautiful. He tells them he will prepare a big house with soft mattresses and clean water for them one day. Because they are worth it.

And then, on the darkest of dark days, when the Teacher is silenced and can paint no more, his friends come unraveled, writhing in grief and numb with disbelief. Slowly they make their way back to the Dumpster where they first encountered him. Some are drunk and disheveled once more. All are paralyzed with sorrow. They stand staring in silence. Someone decides to open the Dumpster. He wants his canvas back and his old pain. After all, it's safe and familiar. Others agree. They begin to climb up so they can lift its heavy lid. But they cannot.

It's locked. "It's locked? Who locks trash? How stupid!" someone yells through angry tears.

But as hard they try, they are unable to open the lid. It has been carefully secured.

With nails.

It is then that they notice Judas' wall of graffiti. Now washed white. On it hangs a portrait of each of them. Clothed. Clean. Full of life and freedom. Teeth straight. Hair combed. Shoulders squared. Wide smiles. The Artist has left them a gallery. They hardly recognize themselves in these gorgeous renderings. But each one finds his portrait and carefully finger-traces his or her new eyes, lips, and jawline. Judas is a no-show, but his portrait hangs here too.

Each one marvels at the mystery. And the memory of his or her smudged canvas languishing in the bottom of the trash bin seems to fade.

Knowing they would return to try and reclaim their pain from the Dumpster, he has left an inscription at the bottom of the wall, beneath the beautiful portraits. It is written in spray paint.

THIS IS WHAT I SEE.

*God didn't go to all the trouble of sending his Son merely to point an accusing finger, telling the world how bad it was. He came to help, to put the world right again. Anyone who trusts in him is acquitted. (John 3:17 MSG)*

## when love sees you
### *jesus*
Lyrics from *Music Inspired by The Story*

Blessed are you, as you weep on your knees,
With perfume and tears washing over my feet,
Blessed are you, beggar, hopeless and blind,
Calling for mercy when I'm passing by.
Blessed are you, shaking your head,
At two tiny fish and some bread,
Blessed are you as you tremble and wait
For the first stone thrown at your sinful disgrace.

Tell me your story,
Show me your wounds,
And I'll show you what Love sees
When Love looks at you.
Hand me the pieces, broken and bruised,
And I'll show you what Love sees
When Love sees you.

Blessed are you, walking on waves,
To find yourself sinking when you look away,
Blessed are you, leper, standing alone,
The fear on their faces is all that you've known.

Blessed are you, lonely widow who gave
Your last shiny coin to Yahweh,
Blessed are you with your silver and lies,
Kissing the One who's saving your life.

I see what I made in your mother's womb.
I see the day I fell in love with you.
I see your tomorrows, nothing left to chance;
I see my Father's fingerprints.
I see your story, I see my name
Written on every beautiful page.
You see the struggle, you see the shame,
I see the reason I came.

I came for your story . . .

*the thief*
# steve and jesus

I LIVE IN a small suburban neighborhood with homes erected about twenty years ago around a good-sized pond. Many of the houses are nuzzled around its shore and have tranquil views of sun-soaked geese honking and ambling along on their webbed waders. Like most bodies of water, our pond begs for long sighs of admiration at dusk, which is where many folks find themselves with a lazy grip on fishing poles, chatting up all sorts of dogs and babies who are taking their grown-ups for a stroll. Our house is situated so that we have to walk down a short little stone path to see actual water, but the payoff is significant when you haven't been spoiled all day by enjoying the view from a kitchen window.

We do this many times a day, my three-year-old and I, while her brother is in school. When I can't put together one more puzzle or make one more donkey out of Play-Doh, we head to the pond to walk and point and play Who Can Spot the Blue Heron First? Lately I haven't been fake-losing much at all.

There are two swans in our pond who are, without a doubt, the most fantastically beautiful creatures I've ever seen (and I think I covered how I feel about birds in an earlier chapter). They are so refined and elegant, gliding without effort across the sunlit glass. I always forget all the work their feet are doing below the surface. There's never any visible trace of exertion, only fluid, unbroken movement. Whenever Pepper and I are walking, one or both of these magnificent creatures paddles all the way across the pond to greet us and then swims alongside while we stroll most of the way around the shore. They've done this since day one.

Initially, it kind of freaked me out. They are so fearless and like to come up so close, and I was worried they might try to snatch Pepper and take her down to their underwater swan lair. (I'm stable like that.) Then I just figured maybe they were waiting for us to pull some Wonder Bread out of our pockets to share with them. I've since learned that while a few rogue residents are packin' bread, the area itself is a registered wildlife sanctuary and feeding anybody anything is strictly prohibited. I've decided the swans aren't after snacks; they just want us to feel warmly greeted, which we do. There's a certain comfort in their company now.

From across the pond (something I like to say in a British accent), they look slight and delicate. But up close, I am always struck by how thick and strong their necks and bodies are. Beauty is almost always underestimated at a distance. I read somewhere that a female swan, like any good mama, can be extremely aggressive when her nest is in peril. So, in addition to underwater lairs, I am always keenly aware of any possible secret swan nests.

The other day, we were taking one of our many treks around the pond with a swan in tow when Pepper stopped and sat down for no real reason right in the middle of the path. I looked closer to see what sort of bug or weed she was inspecting, but she seemed intent on moving around some small stones in a dirt pile. Normally, she likes to toss them in the water, hoping for varying sizes of splash, but today I could see invisible blueprints unscrolling themselves on her forehead, and I knew we weren't going anywhere soon. So I sat down next to her. Swan stopped too . . . patiently treading water.

She played with the rocks for a long time, choosing them carefully, setting them down methodically, and then moving them again. Stacking them a little, and then a little higher, and then leveling all of her careful construction and starting over. When you are three years old, there are only so many times you can start over before determination gives way to frustration, which gives way to a trembling snot fest. She was just about to enter DEFCON 2 when I leaned in to see if I could figure out what it was she was building and how I might help before her tiny fists balled up with rage. Swan looked on.

Whatcha doin, Pep?

I can't, Mama!

Can't what, love?

Make her . . . *herrr*! she moaned.

*Her who?*

She was pointing first at her pile of stones and then at Swan, who suddenly looked a little ashamed.

Glancing at the mound of rocks, I realized she had been trying to fashion a swan out of them. Several small stones made a careful oval for the body. A few larger pointy ones were meant to be the harped wings, I guessed, and the neck was what kept giving her fits. She was trying to stack them on top of one another, clumsily, to achieve the high arch of Swan's neck, bending up and away from its little rock body.

Oh baby, stones don't make good swans, I guess.

Stones can't be swans, Mama, she repeated with resignation and slouched shoulders.

But before I could impart some "if at first you don't succeed" lesson, she was skipping off again. Swan was happy we were on the move once more, paddling alongside my wonderful girl. Pepper fills up every single day with these kinds of noble endeavors. Some of them victories, many of them not, leaving me well rehearsed in both celebration and consolation. But this particular little labor of love left a tightness in my chest. I looked back once or twice at the abandoned stack of stones and allowed her small disappointment to take root in my own heart. It rang true and familiar in a thousand moments of my life.

*Stones can't be swans, Mama.*

This might have been the best description yet of the condition of my heart as I wrestle with the ongoing ache of trying to build something lovely out of my life from dumb rocks on a dirt path.

There are moments when I've wished that I had made a decision to follow Christ as an adult and not as a second grader. Even just now, I had to backspace that sentence three times trying to avoid the easy churchspeak. Follow Christ? Ask Jesus into my heart? Accept Christ? Become a believer? Don't misunderstand me. I am eternally grateful for a childhood marked with biblical instruction and careful guidance from my parents, teachers, pastors, and the like. You can't say enough about a strong foundation. But learning to speak that familiar language of faith at such a young age has left me with a well-worn vocabulary and a listless way of experiencing my own salvation. Lukewarm. I will certainly take credit for my own apathy and for allowing the work of the cross to become distant, sentimental . . . decorative, even.

*When*, I wonder, *did I stop being astonished?*
*Was I ever?*

Or did the honest confession of a child's prayer simply morph into a good kid's dos and don'ts, which eventually bled into teenage Christian school studies that cultivated a young woman who had just a few more questions than answers, which nurtured a songwriter who is so familiar with the vernacular of Christianity she can even make important words rhyme?

This is what I envy sometimes about people who find Jesus later in life. They are so unpolluted by the language of religion that they can only speak in their own native tongue. They are wrecked to pieces to actually discover and then name their sin, and they are nearly destroyed when they first really understand what it cost Jesus to absolve it. They live from the center of true amazement at the gift of a second chance they've been given and not from the sidelines of fatigued familiarity.

I have a pastor friend who told me the best prayer he ever heard was from an old guy who had lived a hard and reckless life and was ready to hand his crusty heart to a Savior. On bended knee in the church office, he announced, "There is zero possible way you could still love me, God . . . but if you do, then holy ****, let's do this."

I want to experience my depravity like that. I don't even remember the last time I was honestly appalled by my own sin. I am so constantly hugging my knees to do a big cannonball jump into the deep end of grace that I forget what it even feels like to stare into my own corruption. As I write this, it's about twenty days into the Lenten season, and my heart wants to prepare for the miracle of Easter. But first it must pass through the dark night of death. First there are things I desperately need to be nailing to the wood.

My thoughts turn toward the thieves who shared Jesus' last few earthly moments. That right there is something to think about. He took his last agonizing breath in the presence of total strangers. The people who had stood with him, traveled with him, broke bread with him, learned from him, cried with him . . . the ones who loved him more than anyone, were either scattered or crumpled beneath his feet, lost in their own sea of pain. Unable to hold him the way we each hope to hold the ones we love in the last moments of their lives.

Gazing up (if they could even stomach it) to see the cracked, parched lips of the One who had spoken every blessing over them. The mangled feet of a servant King who had, only days before, stooped to wash the filth from theirs. Mary, having once touched noses with her wrinkly pink baby, inhaling his perfect newborn breath, would now suffer the agony of watching him be swallowed whole by a remorseless pain. Every mother's worst nightmare: incapacitation.

But while his flesh fades under a steel sky, his heart isn't going anywhere. His physical anguish does not thwart his spirit from continuing his life's work, even now. Loving broken men. Unlocking the vault in the presence of a known thief. Gift-wrapping the jewels.

Even on a cross, sin confuses and polarizes love. One thief cannot accept the unthinkable gift. Lashing out, clawing at grace. Unable to stare into the heart of so much beauty. The other, unable to look away. We have a very short account of Jesus' time with the open-hearted thief, just a few recorded words between them, but we know they must have hung there beside each other, under the angry heavens, for hours and hours. What was said?

I wish we knew his name. Jesus was big on names. I think he would hate that we only know him as The Thief. Imagine if it was not our name that went down in history but the wickedness we were most known by. I don't think Jesus would be happy with that. Anymore than he would want all of us to call you The Liar or to call me The Hypocrite, especially after he made a point to call us sons and daughters. I can imagine that God hears all this "thief" talk and wants to interrupt: "Hey, quit talking about my kid like that. His name is Steve."

I wonder if Steve and Jesus might have been around the same age. Who knows? Maybe they had even crossed paths as children, playing games in the marketplace. Maybe a breathless young Jesus had run up behind unsuspecting Steve and slapped his shoulder as he ran by. TAG! You're it! Maybe Steve had wandered past the temple steps where Jesus was teaching as a child. Elbowing his buddies. Half giggling but partly transfixed by this boy wonder.

Maybe his parents nagged, "Why can't you be more like Joseph's boy?" Maybe Steve sneered and pushed his chair away from the table.

Did the basket of fish and loaves pass through Steve's hands that day and into his belly? Did he sit on a hillside listening to Jesus talk about the meek inheriting the earth and try not to make eye contact? My heart wants to believe that somehow The Thief's life intersected with Jesus' life before they hung slaughtered like beef, side by side, nailed to lumber.

And even in his final moments, I wonder if Steve begged fervently under his breath not to be recognized by Jesus. Too much shame. Too much disgrace to be hanging next to this

Man who had so obviously walked a different path. Who so clearly had no place on this hill. Who was, as Steve had suspected all along, the Son of God.

Did the sinless Messiah squint through one swollen bloody eye until he could barely make out the profile of his neighbor in this nightmare? Did he wait until this man, racked with sobs and agony, took a small breath . . . just enough of a silence to whisper,

Hey.

Hey, Steve . . . I'm with you.

I'm for you.

As unthinkable as it is to imagine death by crucifixion, I can't escape what torture must have been in this man's heart in that moment. The realization that he'd been led there by every choice, every consequence, every sinful ditch he'd passed out in, only to be confronted with more beauty than any one person should ever be expected to gaze upon. Imagine.

You and I have the untold luxury of experiencing that beauty, the forgiveness, the acceptance, and then the U-turn moment. We get to go and live a new abundant life.

Steve had no time left to make his Lord proud. Or impress his parents. He didn't get to hear church members brag about how he'd really turned his life around. He never shared his testimony. He could not offer Jesus any service or effort or earn any badges. He won not a single soul for the kingdom. No mission trips. He never tithed. He witnessed to no one. He studied no Scripture. He wasn't baptized. He was surely the worst performing and least-decorated Christian in history.

And the first one to enter heaven with Jesus.

Is it accidental that the first man to walk into paradise with Christ had zero possibility of imagining he might have earned it?

Even as a child, I've wondered about Steve. Growing up, our family always went to church on Good Friday. I realize now it's because my mom was always the church pianist or the choir director or was involved somehow in church music, so we went whenever she went. The service was never as packed as it was on Easter morning, but a good handful of people usually were in attendance. I always loved the Good Friday service. It was right up my alley. Lots of candlelight. Songs in minor keys. Nobody made you turn and greet your neighbor with donut crumbs stuck in your teeth. There was no snappy offertory number from the choir. No one clapped on the first and third beat. Good Friday service was sacred. Dark and reverential. We were always served Communion, paying extra special attention to the body and blood. Everyone was expected to be quiet afterward, leaving the sanctuary in silence, holding the holy sorrow of that day in our hearts and keeping it there until Sunday.

More than once on Good Friday I considered that I might want to be a monk. A Nazarene girl monk, I guess. Sure, I was only eleven, but I was pretty sure, even then, that the hallowed halls of some monastery were calling me. Only later did it occur to me that I was merely experiencing the early onset of acute introversion. *Let's keep the lights low and the chitchat lower, people. I didn't come here to make friends.* This could be somewhat of a bumper sticker for my life.

Even when I was all grown up and had moved away from home, I almost always found a small church or chapel on Good Friday where I could be quiet with my heart and sit with my lapful of sin, humming the alto line of "O Sacred Head Now Wounded." It was healing and somehow managed to put me back in touch with my need for salvation.

When I moved to LA right after college, I was lost and tired. (And certainly not for the last time in my life.) I had been experiencing a slow and steady erosion of my faith over the last few years. Still banging out the worship choruses on a church piano every Sunday but feeling largely indifferent to any kind of real encounter with Jesus. One night I was coming home around eleven after waiting tables at a pretentious Asian restaurant in Santa Monica when it dawned on me, somewhere in the middle of I-10 eastbound, that it was Good Friday.

Call it nostalgia. Call it guilt. Looking back, I call it the Holy Spirit, but I was overcome with sadness that I hadn't even known what day it was. I'm not even sure I knew it was the month of April, because I was living on such autopilot. By the time I got home, I could barely see the windshield of my car through my tears. To this day, I'm not sure exactly why I was crying. I didn't have any big secret sins to confess. I wasn't having some prodigal return or a Damascus Road moment. I just couldn't stop crying.

I think I just missed the way I had felt on Good Fridays in the past. Like I was carrying around a secret love letter crumpled up and shoved down deep in my pocket that read, "Don't forget how much I love you."

That's what I missed. Being worth something to somebody.

I dragged my tearful, teriyaki-stained self into my dark apartment. My roommate was not home yet, thankfully, so I lit a few candles. Dug my Bible out from under a stack of fashion magazines and went into the kitchen and managed to find a couple of leftover dinner rolls. There was a bottle of wine on the counter too, and I poured myself a glass. I knew I was breaking all kinds of church rules. I don't think twenty-three-year-old waitresses can dip sourdough rolls into cheap merlot and serve themselves Communion and still be in good theological standing. I didn't care. There was only one other person sitting on that floor with me, and he didn't care either. I read through the account of that dark night and the events leading up to it and confessed as many of my sins as I could remember since the previous weekend. I wanted to leave them on the cross like Steve did.

I bet Jesus saw straight into Steve's heart in that moment. Saw the embarrassment. Saw the regret that he couldn't even bow properly before his new King but wanted nothing more. I bet Jesus knew, even in his own agony, that Steve was frantically looking for small stones to stack up. Anything. Anything to pile on top of each other that might just sort of resemble a swan. Trying to remember just one moment in his life he wasn't ashamed of what might pass as somewhat redeeming. Surely.

I'll just stack these up once more, real quick, and try to . . .

Hey.

Hey, Steve . . .

I'm for you.

Stones can't be swans, buddy. Let's keep going.

Almost there . . .

Just close your eyes.

I've got this last mile.

Holding the bread in my mouth and sipping the wine slowly, I climb up there with Steve to remember what it's like to be loved enough that you stop trying to rearrange stones into swans.

Because we are the swan, Steve and me. Perfect. Holy. Made righteous. Beautiful. But strong and a little scary. Paddling furiously along the shoreline and pausing next to anyone else who stops to stack rocks and wonders how we got so white.

◎

*And he said unto Jesus, Lord, remember me when thou comest*
*into thy kingdom. And Jesus said unto him, Verily I say*
*unto thee, Today shalt thou be with me in paradise.*
*(Luke 23:42–43 KJV)*

# how love wins
## *the thief*
### Lyrics from *Music Inspired by The Story*

My life began like any other man,
Held beneath a mother's loving gaze.
Somewhere between now and then
I lost the man I could have been,
Took everything that wasn't mine to take,
But Love believes that it is not too late.

Only one of us deserves this cross,
A suffering that should belong to me.
Deep within this man I hang beside
Is the place where shame and grace collide,
And it's beautiful agony
That he believes it's not too late for me.

This is how Love wins, every single time,
Climbing high upon a tree where someone else
    should die.
This is how Love heals the deepest part of you,
Letting himself bleed into the middle of your wounds.

This is what Love says, standing at the door:
You don't have to be who you've been before.
Silenced by His voice, death can't speak again.
This is how Love wins.

Did you see this moment from the start,
That we would drink this cup of suffering?
I wonder, did we ever meet,
Childhood games in dusty streets?
For all my many sorrows and regrets,
Nothing could compare to just this one:
That in the presence of my King
I cannot fall upon my knees,
I cannot carry you up to your throne.
You instead, will carry me back home.

What can wash away my sin?
Nothing but the blood, nothing but the blood.
What can make me whole again?
Nothing but the blood, nothing but the blood.
Because this is what Love says, standing at the door:
You don't have to be who you've been before.
And silenced by His voice, death can't speak again.
This is how Love wins.

*mary magdalene*
# gemology

YOU'D THINK BY now I would know better than to compile a lofty list of New Year's resolutions. I mean, really. Are we going to actually learn French this year, Nichole? What's that? Cello lessons too? Good. Now let's address the treadmill—iPod case match the new Nikes? Yusss. Let the ball drop in Times Square then. I'm locked and loaded.

I really have put a stop to that insanity, for the most part. I fail often enough without needing to rent space on some internal billboard to advertise the impending face-plant. It's not that I've totally stopped making resolutions. I've just changed the themes somewhat. They are less about self-improvement and more about self-care. And there is a canyon's width of a difference. On December 31 of this past year, I wrote down only three.

1. Be a truth teller. To the world, and to the mirror.

2. Eat at least one vegetable and one fruit a day.

3. When faced with the luxury of free time in front of a television, try and watch a good documentary.

I am having moderate success with all three (except for the first two), but my commitment to TV programming has been an especially resounding success.

Honestly, it was kind of dumb to even make it a resolution, because documentaries are my favorite thing to watch, just like biographies are my favorite thing to read. Guilt-free snooping. Sanctioned curiosity.

A few months ago, after the kids were in bed, I found myself parked on my red couch with a big bowl of vegetables (right), watching a documentary on the National Geographic Channel called *The 400 Million Dollar Emerald*. This is not the kind of documentary I would normally be drawn to. I like people stories. Enigmatic history and adversarial hurdles and the wonder-of-redemption kind of stories. Or leave out the redemption, if you must. I can handle tragedy too. I find that I am particularly open to a gripping story of loss after a few too many hours of Dora the Explorer and that creepy masked fox of an antagonist. But this documentary was not deeply layered or tragic or emotional, so it was uncharacteristic for me to be so drawn into it. Still, I was captivated by the story about this giant emerald. Excavated in Brazil eleven years ago, its subsequent dramatic tale of greed, deception, and beauty remains an ever-present shroud.

The stone itself is called the Bahia Emerald.

Weighing in at over eight hundred pounds and containing 180,000 carats, making one single shard of the emerald about the size of a man's thigh, the stone, in its entirety, is worth more than four hundred million dollars. In the world of emerald mining, it's an absurdity. As local folklore goes, the miners of the stone hauled it away from the mine on a cart drawn by mules that were, on the journey, attacked by jaguars and cobras and spiders (oh my)! The mules did not survive, so the miners were forced to carry it out of the rain forest manually; eventually it was loaded onto a truck bound for Sao Paulo.

I will spare you the two-hour play-by-play, but suffice it to say, the journey of this rare gem since its discovery has been fraught with drama and scandal. It seems that everyone who has even laid eyes on the stone has claimed a hunk of ownership. The owners of the mine got involved, of course, and then American businessmen got involved, and untold others. Currently eight people claim ownership. It has been a convoluted, exhausting mess of an ordeal.

In 2005, the emerald came to the United States and was hidden, for a time, in an abandoned gas station in the desert outside of San Jose. Who looks there? Couldn't have been safer. It even spent some time on eBay. After it changed more hands and went through several failed and questionable transactions and more drama, it ended up locked in an old bank vault in New Orleans, three floors beneath the ground.

Enter, stage right, Hurricane Katrina. The world's most valuable emerald sat in a bank vault under sixteen feet of water for two months. Couldn't have been safer. Utterly unguarded and totally inaccessible.

Today, the Bahia Emerald, one of the most remarkable gems in history, is buried in the evidence room of the LA County Sheriff. There are more claimants than ever, and it seems an insurmountable task to distinguish and determine who might have legal rights to this specimen. Litigation abounds. And so it sits in a crate. May the best man win. Or the shadiest. Or the wealthiest.

Here's the funny thing. It's ugly. It's a big, ugly, inelegant, awkward mass of rock. Search the Internet for Bahia Emerald next time you're bored. Your first thought will be, *I wouldn't pay two bucks for that thing at a garage sale.* The emerald shards are visible (although dirty and dim) but are wedged into this awkwardly cumbersome black boulder, which looks like it belongs at the base of a fake volcano at Mini Golf World. Kryptonite, fallen on hard times and living under a bridge.

The irony, of course, is unavoidable. Everyone wants it. No one really owns it. It is worth everything because there is none other, and it is worth nothing in a locked crate.

I should have told the emerald story at a party I attended recently. And let me tell you, this party needed a good story. Or a good euthanizing. The whole evening was one long and leisurely march toward Dullsville. Here is why I don't normally do parties. Because the second things get awkward and slow, somebody suggests a little icebreaker kind of game. (I flat-out refused to let my friends throw me a bridal shower for this very reason.) Among my least favorite party games is anything involving word association . . . like, "When I say _____, what's the first thing you say?"

The first thing I usually say in my head is, *I don't want to play.* Because the game always starts out deceptively easy and benign and I think, *This'll be a hoot. Fire away.*

Cookies.

"Milk."

Traffic.

"Rush hour."

Flag.

"American."

But then inevitably I end up saying something slightly too revealing and awkward and immediately wish I was helping the caterer clean up the kitchen.

Chocolate.

"Sock drawer."

Library.

"Excessive late fees/card revoked."

Happy place.

"Kendall-Jackson."

Shampoo.

"Special occasion."

It's all fun and games until somebody drowns in two inches of truth serum or chokes on her own foot.

Despite my general misgivings about this kind of "fun," I decided recently it might be interesting to adopt this exercise as a form of internal research as it relates to my own impressions of the Bible characters I'm writing about. I made a friend ask me and record my answers. Here are few:

David.

"Small."

Moses.

"Hair." (*Hair? Thank you, Charlton Heston.*)

Esther.

"Brave."

Paul.

"Silas."

Jesus.

"Water." (*Interesting. Living water? Baptism? Walking on water?*)

Adam.

"Garden."

Mary Magdalene.

"Shame."

Just for fun, I held on to the list to reference as I was writing about these folks. None of them really caught my attention until just now.

Mary Magdalene.

*Shame?*

But that's not at *all* how I feel about Mary Magdalene, I argued with myself. If I'd had even ten seconds to be thoughtful and intentional about word choice, I would have said things like bold, fiercely loyal, humble, grateful, devoted, exceptional, inspirational.

But since this exercise does not grant the luxury of those reflective ten seconds, I had blurted out my one truest word: *shame*.

I knew I wasn't alone in that reaction. In AD 600 Pope Gregory (the Great) clearly identified Mary Magdalene with sexual sin, suggesting that she was, indeed, the same woman upon whom Jesus imparted forgiveness and compassion. Go and sin no more.

I grew up with that understanding, didn't you? When I was young and first learning to identify Bible characters with certain themes, I knew absolutely that she had been a prostitute. I had no idea what *prostitute* meant, exactly, but I knew she had done some bad things with men and felt so awful about it that she busted open her nicest bottle of Love's Baby Soft perfume and poured it all over the feet of Jesus, drying them with her hair.

This seemed to be the repentant behavior of someone who had really, really messed up, and whatever this prostitute business was, was serious. I knew exactly how she felt too, because I had wanted to crawl into a hole when I cheated on the spelling test, and I would have washed Mrs. Hoyt's shoes with my ponytail for all of recess if it helped that yucky feeling go away.

So I totally understood where she was coming from on the whole prostitute thing.

Yes, there it was, clear as day. Shame. (Interesting, I think, that the first thing I said about Adam was *garden*, but *shame* belongs to Mary.)

In the late 1960s, the Vatican recanted, acknowledging, in effect, that this was a flawed declaration. Nowhere in Scripture is there evidence of Mary's being a prostitute, but sadly (like a tiny footnote correction on the editor's page of a magazine), the initial weight of the accusation left too deep an imprint on the collective imaginations of believers. So she will always be a prostitute. A forgiven prostitute certainly, but a woman who remains stuck in those shadows.

Obviously, judging by my gut-level word choice, under deep layers of my subconscious, Mary still wears the sweater of shame and will probably always be the patron saint of prodigal daughters. Even now in many communities the world over, beautiful rehabilitative programs have sprung up to embrace women who desperately seek relief and restoration from lives lived on the street, and many of them are named Magdalene houses.

The scandal continues, surrounding Mary's shadowy place in New Testament history. I certainly will not try to interpret the darker whispers about her relationship with Jesus. *The Last Temptation of Christ* not only promoted her as a prostitute but insinuated Jesus as a possible customer. *The Da Vinci Code* sought to unravel the mystery behind her clandestine role as his wife and mother of their child. Scholars, cynics, movie producers, best-selling authors, and plenty of regular folks have rubbed their itchy fingers together for ages, hoping to peek behind the curtain to see if there is more to be known about her than what we know. I'm neither qualified nor interested enough to weigh in.

There is only one place I want to meet Mary. In front of the empty tomb.

I have had little trouble placing myself in the lions' den with Daniel or in a jail cell with Paul or on a hill, slaying giants next to David. I have found it to be meaningful and gratifying to attempt to meet them on their emotional home court and then go wrestle with and write about any takeaway moments in my own life.

But the tomb? How could one moment be so universally significant and still so deeply personal? A moment so saturated with hope and redemption that it changed not only the entire face of history but also the trajectory of my own lost heart. The moment that changed everything for every limping, weary pilgrim or arrogant fatheaded Pharisee since. The moment of ancient prophecy fulfilled. The moment where love actually, and not just hypothetically, does win.

I can only put my pen down. How do you comment on a moment that defies commentary?

How could a dictionary contain, between its covers, the words we need to tell that story? To describe the indescribable?

Even the Gospel accounts fall flat for me, I suppose because Scripture is restricted by the same dictionary and the authors had the same inadequate vocabulary we all do. But that does not keep us from attempting to string together words that are clumsy and scarce and anemic in light of the glory of the risen Lord.

I walk with Mary on the path approaching the tomb.

Actually, in my mind, I walk behind her a ways. First, because I find it entirely plausible that she will collapse, midstride, in a crumpled heap, and might need someone to catch her on the way down. But also because her grief is so thick and consuming, she might prefer to be isolated with whatever is left of her heart. I don't want to be tempted to rub her back or whisper gentle encouragement that he would want her to go on and live a full life. So I lag behind a bit.

As we walk, I remember that Jesus, as a baby, was presented with precious gifts from traveling Magi who had come to bear witness and behold the Promised One. Gifts, spices, and oils reserved for royalty. A King has come. Wise men should anoint him.

And on the dark night of sacrifice, when it was finished and Jesus' body had been taken down from the cross, Nicodemus came with about seventy-five pounds of spices and oil, far more than was necessary for one body, scholars say. But not near enough for God's Son. Nicodemus, who had shared his deepest doubts that night about spiritual rebirth, must surely have let his own tears mingle with the aloe and myrrh as he washed and wrapped his beloved Jesus. *My teacher is gone. His student should anoint him.*

Trailing behind the women on the path to the tomb, stooped in sorrow, I see that Mary, too, has brought more spices and oils. Probably unnecessary after Nicodemus and Joseph had been so careful and attentive in the embalming. But she brought them still. Maybe to show added respect and honor?

*He lies lifeless in a cold cave and should not be alone. I will stay with him. My best friend is dead. My hands will anoint him.*

And yet, while I understand their significance, the burial spices confuse me a little in Mary's hands. She must have known she would not have access to his body. While many of the disciples had fled the scene of the crucifixion in fear, Mary had stayed until the bitter end. She had watched the body come down, knew he had been taken into the care of Joseph and Nicodemus, placed in a tomb that was secured with a heavy stone. Surely she had gotten word that Pilate had ordered a guard to be placed there, permitting no one's entrance. (Not having considered anyone's exit.) So what exactly was she hoping to do with the spices?

Did she stand on the other side of the stone, tear-streaked cheeks, palms pressed up against the cold, rough surface of the rock that stood between her and the one moment she really wanted? One more good-bye. She had to have known she wouldn't get past the stone or the guard and into the actual tomb. Maybe she thought she would just anoint herself with the burial spices and hope to lie down and die as close to him as possible.

Why must the most precious jewels be hidden in rock?

A diamond in coal.

An emerald in a massive ore deposit.

Hope entombed behind impenetrable stone.

To excavate that treasure, one must be willing to lose a lot in the process. I couldn't help but think of how Jesus quarried treasure in Mary's life as well as I learned about the process the giant emerald would have to go through in order to be of any real value. An emerald cutter spends a long time examining the rough stone. Inspecting it from all angles, deciding with the newly decreed owner where exactly to make the cuts and harvest the most beautiful gems inside. First, he cuts the basic shape and then the facets. The inside of the emerald is where the fewest flaws are, so a good cutter (and of course we would summon only the best) knows he will lose up to 70 percent of the emerald to find the most beautiful gem deep within.

I suspect he sees in that ugly mass of rock something akin to what Jesus saw in Mary. Surely she had never been loved the way Jesus loved her. Not by her parents or her friends or a lover, if she had any. He saw in her immeasurable value. A gnarled mass of rock and gem worth tunneling through untold walls of mineral deposits to harvest. Turning her around in his hand, holding her up to the light, he looked for her hidden beauty. Planning with specific precision how he would carefully cut into her heart and life, separating her from what could be lost and what should be forsaken, the demons that had to go, the tears that had to be dried, the sickness that needed healing, until he finally held a jewel of untold worth. In the hands of any other, she was unremarkable. In the hands of Jesus, her beauty is blinding.

There had to have been so many competing voices in those frantic days following the crucifixion. The private and paralyzing sorrow of Jesus' closest companions, terrified to be seen publicly, knowing the hunt for their allegiance had begun. The streets were buzzing with news and gossip. News of the crucifixion. Have you heard? Have you heard? News of Judas' suicide. Have you heard? Peter denying any knowledge of Jesus altogether. Have you heard?

Maybe Mary set out on that path with burial spices she could not use simply to escape the cacophony of chaos that swirled around her following Jesus' death. Maybe there was no other way to be alone and quiet with her grieving heart. Maybe her ears were ringing with the din of confusion and disorder left in the wake of Friday's agony.

But she would not find rest from the confusion. An empty tomb awaited her, multiplying her grief in a matter of seconds.

I watch from a distance as she races frantically inside and out. Back in. Back out. Pushing down small sobs that are lodged somewhere in the part of her voice she can no longer access.

To take him from her while he lived was unthinkable. To take him from her in death too was sheer evil.

I watch her fall. Growling in anguish. Rocking back and forth with fists balled into her stomach, trying to push down the pain. The din of noise she hoped to escape was now living in her own head. He's gone??? Where? Have you heard?

Labor pains come in waves, allowing a woman to catch her breath to prepare and bear down again. Grief is no respecter of breath. It is one merciless and unyielding contraction.

And then in the confusion, a voice.

Why are you crying? Who are you looking for?

The gardener! I watch her race over, pleading, every last

ounce of self-restraint keeping her from clutching two fistfuls of robe and shaking him. They've taken my Lord! What have you done with him?? Have you heard? Have you heard?

He speaks again. One word.

Mary.

And she knows then, not by sight but by the sound of her own name coming from his lips, that it is Jesus.

A great cry rises up from her belly.

A great cry falls down from heaven's throne room.

A great cry shakes my own small heart to its foundations.

He's alive.

*HAVE YOU HEARD??*

I do not know why Jesus chose to appear to Mary first instead of to another friend or disciple. I'd like to believe it was because she held Jesus with such a beautiful and fragile heart, and because he knew she would be the best one to deliver the news to the others. Perhaps she knew, more than anyone, how easily broken love can be, and how easily mended.

Surely Jesus saw in Mary what she could never have seen in herself. Believing this, it's easy to imagine Jesus eagerly agreeing to participate in my word-association game.

Mary.

"Perfect."

Mary.

"Loved."

Mary.

"Forgiven."

Mary.

"Treasured."

Mary.

"Mine."

Go ahead and get out a permanent marker and write your own name over Mary's. Then read the list aloud. Have you heard?

*The angel said to the women, "Do not be afraid; for I know that you are looking for Jesus who has been crucified. He is not here, for He has risen, just as He said." (Matthew 28:5-6 NASB)*

## alive
### *mary magdalene*
#### Lyrics from *Music Inspired by The Story*

Who but you could breathe and leave a trail
    of galaxies?
And dream of me?
What kind of Love is writing my story until
    the end with Mercy's pen?
Only you.
What kind of king would choose to wear a crown that
    bleeds and scars to win my heart?
What kind of Love tells me I'm the reason he can't stay
    inside the grave?

You. Is it you?
Standing here before my eyes?
Every part of my heart cries

Alive! Alive! Look what Mercy's overcome.
Death has lost, and Love has won.
Alive! Alive!
Hallelujah, risen Lord,
The only One I fall before.
I am his because he is alive.

Who could speak and send the demons back from
    where they came
With just one Name?
What other heart would let itself be broken every time
    until he healed mine?

You. Only you
Could turn my darkness into dawn running right into
    your arms.

Emmanuel, the promised King,
The baby who made angels sing,
Son of Man who walked with us,
Healing, breathing in our dust,
The author of all history,
The answer to all mysteries,
The Lamb of God who rolled away the stone in front
    of every grave.

*the disciples*
# how to set a table

FEW THINGS SPEAK to people like a good meal.

I know this to be true in my own life as I consider food to be my primary love language. I have read that very insightful book by Gary Chapman about figuring out how to speak the love language your mate longs to hear.[1] Once this happens, unicorns start showing up to slide down the multitude of rainbows that appear. I'm joking. It's a fantastic book, helpful in many family dynamics, too, except for being just a tad narrow in scope due to the missing language of food.

This particular love language might help explain why I am such a disaster in relationships. I have yet to meet someone who really speaks Brie. I mean, convincingly. Sure let's spend time together. Let's use affirming words. Flowers and gifts are fine, but if you walk in with a bouquet of cheese, things are gonna go very well for you.

I bought an enormous cookbook last year entitled *One Big Table* by Molly O' Neill, a former food columnist for the *New York Times* who spent ten years chasing down and dispelling the rumor that the majority of Americans no longer cook at home.[2] It is an astounding 864-page invitation to pull up a chair around this great country's diverse table, and I am making my way through it slothfully and with great delight. Who wouldn't want a generations-old hummus recipe by a woman named Afaf Shaheen? Or to learn how to make perfect short ribs from a gal named Bessie, who describes herself as a "decent barrel racer"?

Every marvelous part of this collection points way beyond the recipes and interesting stories to the larger idea that it's not about the actual food on the table. It's about what the moment means to those seated around it.

Think about our social lives. When somebody is born, we bring food. When somebody dies, we bring food. When somebody gets married, we have food catered. When somebody is in the hospital, we organize food delivery for the family. When someone has a birthday, we meet for dinner to celebrate. When someone breaks our heart, we face-plant large sausage calzones alone. Others do, I mean. I've heard about that happening before to people.

Despite my foodie confessions, I recently completed a ten-day water-only cleansing fast. I do this a couple times a year to allow my body to reboot and to recover a little from the perverse nutritional neglect I subject it to the rest of the year. Without a doubt the most challenging part of a fast for me is never hunger. It's that my social life perishes in a nanosecond because when people gather, food is almost always involved.

Maybe that's why I've always felt deeply emotional about the Last Supper. There are few moments in the New Testament that touch me as deeply as that last meal Jesus shared with his close friends and disciples. I think the most heartbreaking part of the story is that the disciples didn't quite understand what was unfolding. They couldn't possibly grasp the significance of this meal the way we do now. My heart always watches the Last Supper peeking through spaces between fingers clamped over my eyes. It's like watching a movie in which the director lets us in on the fact that the bridge is out a mile up ahead while our lead actor is playing thumb percussion on the steering wheel, hair whipping in the wind on an afternoon drive.

Jesus had gathered his friends in the upstairs guest room of a house to observe the Passover meal, which they probably had shared together several times before. In addition to honoring this long-standing custom, I picture them enjoying hearty conversation, the kind that is born in safe and familiar company. Maybe they unpacked the day's events. Tried to listen and bear each other's burdens. Confessed their big and small failures. Laughed. Gave each other a hard time. Told exaggerated fishing tales, like guys will do. Maybe this felt like Thursday night men's small group.

In my senior year of high school, my Bible teacher served our class a traditional Passover meal as part of our Old Testament studies. In passing around the many different courses, he explained the important symbolism for each.

Bitter herbs to represent the slavery of the Hebrew people, an egg to represent life, a piece of roasted lamb to remember the sacrifices made. Many more elements than I can recall. I admired how important the details were to the Jewish people. Without meaning any disrespect, it seemed like a pretty high-maintenance meal but one that came with a script and specific succession of courses that each disciple would likely have known since boyhood.

I see the disciples there, with their freshly scrubbed heels and toes, noshing and chatting, until at once they feel the tone in the room change. They elbow and shush one another with full mouths and nod in the direction of Jesus, who announces, almost without warning, that one of them will betray him. One of *them*. The men gathered around the table.

You can almost feel the oxygen get sucked out of the story; a thick blanket of nameless anxiety settles over the room. Judas is identified. Judas leaves.

More confusion. Blank stares.

What happens next could have happened on a hillside or in a boat or on a dusty road. But instead, Jesus chose a place he knew would pull them back many times to nurse their broken hearts after the horror of the next forty-eight hours to come. He chose a table.

Typical of Jesus, he meets the disciples right where they are—stuffing their faces. In the middle of the laborious and complex Passover meal, Jesus clears his throat and interrupts with a radical menu change. Chef's special: Two items only.

Bread and wine. Was he, even then, trying to turn their attention from the disciplined detail of the law toward the reckless simplicity of his love? He chooses common items that were easy to remember, easy to find, easy to share.

I wonder if he knew that the siege of grief in the coming days might give away to dissension and stress between his friends. Anticipating that, maybe he knew a meal would level the playing field. It's hard to fight with someone when you're sharing food. Chewing and swallowing don't lend themselves naturally to competition.

I wonder, too, if he glanced into the future and thought of us. Knowing that in all of our progressive sophistication we would need an organic place from which to remember. Flour and grape. Elements that can't really be bettered or modernized.

Several years ago, our family participated in an Angel Tree program around Christmastime. It was set up in the great hall of the Episcopal church we attended then and featured a massive tree dripping with paper ornaments on which had been written the needs of kids, adults, and families in our community.

I've always loved this tradition. Our family had been financially blessed that year, so we decided to go a little crazy with the Angel Tree. We chose an ornament that had an entire family listed on it. They were Hispanic, and the list of names included a grandmother and very small children and every generation in between, including aunts, uncles, cousins, and in-laws. I think there were almost ten people total listed on the ornament we chose. Next to the name of the youngest boy, the same age as my own, were his two Christmas wishes: underpants and a robot. Except robot had been crossed out. I imagined that maybe his grandmother, feeling great indignity about asking for anything at all, had insisted only on listing what the family needed most, nothing more. Robots need not apply.

On shopping day, I was sitting in my driveway, chewing the end of my pencil and trying to organize the large list into manageable categories when I came across the Christmas request from the father of the family. An electric can opener. There was some small note written about arthritis and difficulty using the manual kind.

I sat on the soft leather of my SUV, toasty on the seat warmers, with James Taylor crooning about chestnuts in the background, and started to bawl. This man's one and only Christmas wish was an electric can opener. I pulled myself together and headed to a superstore that would give me the most bang for my buck. After the cart was full with every pair of underwear and bar of soap and can opener that had been requested, I grabbed another cart for all the fun stuff I was dreaming about but was not on the list.

There I was. All dimples and rosy nosed, like Santa, shoving this massive cart through the toy section. My heart was literally leaping out of my chest trying to picture this family's Christmas morning. It took three store employees to help me get everything out to my car. That night, I slept deeper and more peacefully than I had in a long time.

I called the church coordinator the following day to figure out what the next step was. She said we could either drop the items off at the church, or she could give us the address of the family if we'd like to deliver the gifts ourselves.

Take it to the actual family? Like . . . personally?

This was my response, almost verbatim:

*(Long silence.)*

*Oh. Ummm.*

*Ya know . . . uh . . . I think . . . it's just that we're really not . . . Um.*

*Delivery seems potentially . . . I dunno . . . it could get sort of, maybe . . .*

*It's just, you know how crazy the holida . . .*

*I mean, I'd hate for the family to feel any . . . ya know . . . well . . .*

*Fine. What's the address?*

Oddly enough, the church lady did absolutely nothing to rescue me from any of the silence. In that moment, I was kicking myself for not just writing a check and letting someone else shop and deliver and get a sweat moustache because they couldn't remember anything from high-school Spanish.

We piled in the car a few days before Christmas, said a prayer, and headed to a run-down apartment complex tucked away in a low-rent part of Dallas. We couldn't even tell them we were coming. They had no phone. And what would I have said? *Hola!* Muchas presents and awkward gringos en route!

We decided a proper introduction was necessary before

we barfed Christmas all over their apartment. We got to their door on the top floor after navigating a complicated labyrinth of stairs and walkways, and knocked twice. Grandmother answered. I smiled. She smiled. We said, "Merry Christmas!" She said, "Okay." Then I started down the dreadful path of ummms and errrrs and mortifying hand gestures involving robots and toilet paper and then finally I just held up a finger said, "One minute, please. Be right back."

And with that, we made trip after trip after trip after trip to and from our car, unloading endless bags and boxes into an apartment the size of my garage, where ten people lived. Once everything was loaded in, one of their children stepped forward, Mara, age ten, and much to our surprise, spoke broken but beautiful English. She started translating for Grandmother while all the wide-eyed family members stood staring in disbelief at the boxes and bows.

"My grandmother says her heart aches with happiness. She applied for the church tree but did not expect anything to happen and did not tell us. She says you have brought sunshine into our home. She does not know how to thank you."

I turned and looked at Grandmother, who had a great many fresh tears on her leathered cheeks. I moved across the room and embraced her. We just cried together for a few seconds, and I felt so grateful that we had delivered these gifts ourselves. We repeatedly waved off the suggestion that they needed to repay us somehow. We prepared to leave, carrying full hearts inside us.

Because I love words so much, they rarely fail me. But my words were in the wrong language this time and of little use to me in saying good-bye. We turned to leave, and my husband and son were smiling and waving at everyone, and for some inexcusably awkward reason, I started backing up slowly toward the door, bowing to each individual like I was at a kimono convention in Tokyo.

We were juuust about out the door, when the lovely Mara started translating again.

"My grandmother asks me for your phone number, please."

I froze.

"Mmmmmkaaaaay . . . ," I said slowly. I took her pencil and hovered over the paper for a few seconds, asking if God would understand if I gave them a fake number because I really don't need a ten-member Hispanic family project right now, because God, you know I am very busy and important, and we have gone above and beyond with this little Christmas gesture, and my work here is done, people.

I heard the distinct sound of God's eyes rolling.

So I wrote down our real phone number with more than a little regret, and off we went. I lay in bed that night staring at the ceiling, certain that a boundary had been breached. I had allowed the line between generosity and accessibility to be crossed, and now Grandmother was not going to rest until she had our flat-screen TV. Give 'em an inch, ya know?

How typical of God's enemy. To paralyze and scramble our brains with a total self-serving fear until we've married the words *different* and *dangerous* in an inseparable union. Lots of bloodshed on our small planet and in our own country has been rooted in this very simple lie.

Sure enough, a few days later, the phone rings. It is sweet Mara, calling from a pay phone (sent to do the dirty work, I guessed). I let her get through her thank-you speech about her lip gloss and backpack, and all the while I'm just waiting for the big gimme. Waiting for the real reason for her call as I sat stewing in my own toxic brew of cynicism. *(Just write the check next year, dummy.)*

Finally, she manages to say, "Um. Mrs. Nichole, the real reason I'm calling is" (*Uh-huh, here we go.*) "because my grandmother wanted me to ask" (*Yup. Spit out the dollar figure, sweetie.*) "if your family could please come back to our home for dinner. To receive our thanks."

Silence.

*Dinner.*

More silence.

*(Dontcrydontcrydontcry.)*

Clearing throat.

"What time?"

I hung up, nearly suffocating from the shame.

Three weeks later we were standing in that same tiny apartment. Every relative and evidently half the block had shown up to receive us like dignitaries. The women had on fresh lipstick and stood to one side of the room. The men held their ball caps in their hands and stood on the other side.

Countless children sat cross-legged on the floor, perfectly behaved. A small card table was set up in the middle of the room with three folding chairs for myself, Errol, and Charlie. Grandmother motioned for us to please sit down.

Then, at her order, dinner was presented to us with great fanfare and hustle. Simple food. Rice and beans. A plate of boiled chicken drumsticks with a brownish sweet sauce I didn't recognize. I know it would make a better story if I told you how incredible this humble meal was. Truthfully, it didn't taste good at all to us. There were strange side dishes, mysterious and unfamiliar, and not in a good way. Errol and I, understanding what was at stake, ate voraciously. Rubbing our bellies, grinning widely, asking for thirds. We shared a warm can of Orange Crush between us. Even Charlie was mercifully quiet for a child who tells the painful truth about everything with a megaphone. He kept happily scooping up rice until he hopped down to play with the new robot and a friend he couldn't understand but didn't need to.

I figured once we had finished eating, the rest of the room would begin to help themselves. But nobody moved. They just watched us. Smiling. Nodding. Bearing witness. And then they filed quietly out the door.

I have never felt so deeply honored in my life.

All that was good and right and beautiful in the world was sitting in front of me in greasy pools on a paper plate. Everything pure and selfless and true was balanced here on a wobbly card table. And I didn't want to get up.

This is how it feels when someone serves you from a pure and true place inside. This is why, I believe, Jesus gathered his beloved around a table and not on the shore of a lake or on the steps of the synagogue. He wanted to serve them. To pull them under his wing for one more precious night before the nightmare began, and to gently encourage them to remember him as often as they gathered to eat. And because they were family, I'm guessing that was fairly often.

After his resurrection, Jesus finds his friends gathered again in their room. Several reports now had leaked in about different sightings of their teacher and Lord, and they were surely filled with both a frantic new hope and a terrifying reluctance to trust in it. As the room buzzes with debate and various reports, Jesus sneaks in and shows himself to them.

Why do you look so troubled? It's me! I told you! Touch me if you need to, so you believe it. (And then miraculously . . . ) Do you have anything to eat?

He returns again to the table.

The first three times Jesus appears to his followers after his death, he does it over a meal. On the road. In a room. By the shore. Remember. Remember. Remember.

And then specifically to Peter: If you love me, feed my lambs. Feed their bellies. Fill the cavern in their hearts. Take care of my sheep.

The table of Christ has as many chairs as the planet has people.

Each of us holds a standing invitation to sit and stay and feed our souls on the extravagance and nourishment laid out before us. We are ushered to our seats with Grandmother's great haste and happiness. Heaven lines the walls to watch. The disciples left some crumbs on the chairs before us, but there's plenty more. The kitchen never closes.

The Last Supper is sacred because it's where we first learned to remember together a broken Body, a river of blood, the transaction that purchased our meal ticket.

But remembering together can be difficult if there is no place to gather.

And gathering will always be for tables.

*When the day of Pentecost came, they were all together in one place. Suddenly a sound like the blowing of a violent wind came from heaven and filled the whole house where they were sitting.*
*(Acts 2:1–2)*

# empty
## *the disciples*
### Lyrics from *Music Inspired by The Story*

All my devotion and misguided loyalty,
Swinging my sword in the garden while you pray
    for your enemies,

All my allegiance, I loved you and you alone,
But who'd believe that I could mean it now that
    the rooster crowed?
Now we're huddled up here, trying to swallow our fear.
We still smell the bread and wine, hear your words
    running through our minds,
Holding our breath now, for what comes next now,
Holding out for some kind of sign.

But there's an empty cross, there's an empty tomb,
Fire and wind now sweeping in this tiny upper room.
There's a hungry world, there's a risen King.
Unlock the doors, what reason more could we ever
    need?
So sing with me, I dare you to,
There's an empty cross, there's an empty tomb.

We wept from a distance, watched pieces
    of our dreams
Buried with you, every last wound, sealed with stone,
    beyond our reach.
Sweet, sweet Jesus, every question, every fear,
Vanishing, like vapor dreams now that you're
    standing here.

Now the tears come easy, when you say you're
    leaving.
We touched the place the nails went through,
Wanting one more day with you,

But it's good-bye now, for a little while now,
Believing everything you said is true.

We will sing this song
To make your name live on,
Until every heart hears of the way you rescued us.

*paul*

# when to cut class

I LIVE IN a gray world, spiritually speaking. I have trouble now with the same neatly stacked, clearly labeled boxes that once brought me great comfort and security. Sometimes, in matters of faith, I feel like I walk alone in this middle gray. Like a nervous adolescent, suspended between dollhouses and diaries. Wishing again for a sweet, unblemished faith beneath a safely hung moon.

The book of Revelation is saturated with dreams and metaphors both fantastical and terrifying. It's rich with prophecy and prediction, and open to interpretation both generously subjective or rigorous and literal. Probably suffering in the hands of either extreme. God summons an angel to tell John to tell us that bad stuff is about to go down, and soon. He addresses many specific churches about their specific sin. Churches no longer found on modern maps. Churches hard to pronounce or having way too many vowels, like Laodocia, for instance. But despite the carefully identified audience, you and I are also invited to listen soberly, tucking the same warnings away in our hearts and attempting to unearth their meanings.

For those of us who have grown up in the church, there are certain passages in Revelation that linger over a lifetime. For me, they linger mostly because I associate them with terrible fear.

I remember two things about the fourth grade. First, my teacher, Mrs. Houtz, introduced me to *A Wrinkle in Time* by Madeleine L'Engle, changing the way I saw ideas and words on a page forever. Second, our small Christian school thought it would be a swell idea to show us a movie in chapel one afternoon called *A Thief in the Night*. A rip-roaring adventure about a nice suburban family who does not get airlifted with Jesus in the Rapture but crawls through all manner of fresh new hell that greets them each morning in Left-Behind Land. Helicopters chasing people over bridges. People vanishing in the middle of everyday activities. A lawnmower still inching across the lawn with no one pushing it. Terrifying images that burrow into the imagination of a child and take root over time. So began my courtship and eventual messy, scandalous, full-blown affair with fear. So also began my great confusion about fear's sworn enemy, God's love.

There is a famed passage in Revelation's third chapter, where the Laodocian church is warned that its sin is the worst kind of the worst. It's apathetic. Not hot. Not cold. But the dreaded lukewarm temperature that's worthy only of being spit out of God's own mouth. *The Message* translates it as, "You make me want to vomit."[1]

Now there's a terrifying image: being spit out, with

contempt, from God's own mouth. Spitting is for curses. Spitting is a sign of disrespect and disgust. This is more than unsettling, and not just for fourth graders. The very word *lukewarm* can rouse panic in the heart of most Christians.

In my humble opinion, this is the same fear that motivates and informs so much of modern evangelicalism. From this passage, and others like it, an ideology is born. A brand of "take no prisoners" faith emerges. A battle cry goes up, uniting large numbers of people who, arms linked, move across the landscape of culture and politics and art. Putting stakes in the ground. Congratulating each other on our Sold Outness. Everything black or white. Hot or cold. No danger of lukewarm allegations. Nobody's gonna make God vomit on our watch.

Genuine conviction? For many, absolutely. And I will respect that. Wobbly conviction swept up in an emotional current and drenched in fear? For many others, yes. Fear that if we don't holler loud enough . . . Or take a stand enough . . . And fill up arenas enough . . . And be extreme enough, and take back our country enough, and draw enough lines in enough sand, in the end we might not be . . . enough.

We might be spit out. On the day of judgment, we could be herded off with the goats to the left side of Jesus while the sheep move right. God help us if, at the end of a life marked with evidence of good, solid Christian effort, he actually says, I knew you not.

Fear.

While not everyone is motivated by this nervousness, it has been true for me personally. I've got hard calluses from jostling around on the back of so many bandwagons. Saying things from a stage I would never have said in a conversation, only because I knew what would make a certain crowd cheer with approval. Repeating certain catch phrases. Reading my part of the dutiful script in an interview. Tossing my head back to laugh at political jokes that are not only offensive but, as far as jokes go, aren't even clever. Taking firm stands and hard lines on things that I don't feel firmly in my heart of hearts, all out of the deep fear of sounding lukewarm. This makes me not a "sold-out Christian" but one who's selling out. In a panic that somehow these many gray places in my faith will be sniffed out by the Wishy-Washy Patrol.

All of this personal and fearful baggage finds me pulling up a chair across the table from the apostle Paul. If I'm honest, I'm not quite sure what we'll talk about. He always seems to have a lot to say; I just don't know what to do with a bunch of it. We decide to break the ice by chatting first about his famous name change.

Saul (as he was first known) has a pretty astonishing story. He's a very well-educated guy, schooled especially in the law of Moses. He is devout and deadly serious about his faith and heritage, defending sacred texts and principles with fierce conviction. It is his life's work. He aligns himself with an equally refined and rigid legalistic group called the Pharisees. The same Pharisees that become Exhibit A in many of the talks and sermons Jesus gave.

As in: See that well-meaning bunch over there parading around all their holy nonsense, flying the great flag of Self? Yeah, Exhibit A. Pretty much do the opposite of what those guys do, okay?

Imagine what an insulting slap that must have been in the face of a Pharisee. How condescending for a nobody like Jesus to openly criticize you on your own turf. Educating people about what the law is *really* trying to say. And then adding a bunch of new stuff nobody's ever even heard of.

Imagine that you, a professor with tenure at Harvard Divinity School, have a double PhD in history and religion. Your students are bright and inquisitive, and you have great hope for their futures. One day, a good handful of them start cutting class to go to sit on the floor of the cafeteria and listen to the head janitor lecture instead. They're taking notes and asking questions about life and God, transfixed by what they're hearing, until pretty soon the whole campus seems absurdly in love with the stupid custodian. To make matters worse, he's distorting the truth! And then he starts handing out fish sticks and Tater Tots, and people are, like, losing their minds over him.

You gather for an emergency meeting with your colleagues. Dumbstruck. Incensed. Something must be done! Clearly the janitor must go. (Are we really even *having* this conversation??) He's simply got to go. All in favor?

But then, once the janitor is taken care of for good, things get worse for this esteemed institution and its educators. The cafeteria is now bustling with activity and energy and . . . what's this? A growing agenda. Very few students are coming to class to learn anymore. They just seem to stand around, comforting and inspiring each other with stories about the janitor. The way he loved them. The way he spoke tenderly to each of them. Never yelling at anybody for letting the frozen yogurt machine leak all over the place. He was more than just a janitor, they're saying. After a while, the students decide to take his message to other campuses. Yale, Brown, even a bunch of local community colleges, any place with a cafeteria. It becomes a groundswell. It becomes unstoppable.

And Professor Saul starts to unravel. He will not stand idly by and watch people distorting and spreading their own version of nonsense, running around recklessly polluting Judaism. Bastardizing truth. And so, one day this highly educated, well-regarded man just snaps. He moves deftly from dorm room to dorm room, hauling people out by their hair, locking them up, dragging them into the center of campus to stone them. Blood drips from his hands, fueling his rage. God would approve! This foolishness must be extinguished! Students are horrified; they run. He chases after them, the cocoon of his anger wrapping itself around him, overcoming him until he emerges as a full-blown terrorist.

Framing it like this helps me have compassion for him. It helps me understand the internal spiral of a man whose original sin was really misguided devotion. He was in love with himself, his intellect, his understanding of what he believed the whole picture of truth to be. So devoted was he, in fact, he believed God needed defending. And he felt his only recourse was to scare people back into submission. Fear begets fear. Nobody was going to accuse *him* of being lukewarm.

Of course, the best part of Professor Saul's story takes place in the middle of a dirt road on his way to Damascus. He's back on the hunt. Moving, in his madness, to the next campus to purge and cleanse its drifters of their disloyalty, when a light penetrates the sky, brilliant and intense, disabling him completely. He is literally robbed of his sight and knocked to the ground. Vulnerable. Unarmed. Terrified. And then the light speaks:

Saul, why are you hurting me?

Trembling, he asks, who are you??

I am Jesus, the One you persecute.

In an instant, he understands the heartbreaking truth that he has been hunting the very One he believed himself to be defending. God and God's Son. The God of Abraham and Jacob. The God of his everything. The same God that lures people out of ivory towers to eat off of a filthy cafeteria floor.

It's true, Saul whispers. He was more than a janitor.

He remains blind for three full days (always an interesting number in the New Testament in discussions about the journey from death to life). Truth illuminates. Truth exposes darkness to light. But death doesn't like to die in daylight.

Death likes to die in shadows. And Saul had some dying to do. I don't believe his ongoing blindness was a punishment. I believe it was required reflection.

It's interesting how the term *Damascus Road experience* gets tossed around, implying that one could be instantly seized and transformed by the floodlights of Jesus. Change course in a nanosecond, like Saul. But we forget about the three days of blindness. We forget that he had to sit in isolation without seeing a thing so that he might see everything. I think the light was to incapacitate him, but the shadows that followed were where the real change took place.

We want everything instantly. As new creatures, we cling to the promise that the old has passed away, and it has. But I believe God lets a little scar tissue linger, and maybe a trace of a limp, so that our brokenness may always point to him. Maybe Paul regained his sight fully but lost a scorched eyebrow that day. Just enough for people to see him coming and say, "Whoa. You're *that* guy?"

When my dad was about four years old, he and his younger brother were obsessed with playing cowboys. I look at my own boy now, climbing a tree or flying down the driveway on his bike, a sword strapped to his back, rounding up invisible bad guys, and I try to picture my dad. How could such a larger-than-life man, my hero, my rock, the strongest and safest arms I know, have ever been a plastic-gun-toting little cowboy? It's baffling.

As the story goes, Dad climbed into my grandpa's closet

one afternoon and helped himself to a pair of suit pants, grabbed some sewing shears, found a sneaky place to hide, and got busy making himself some cowboy fringe.

"Someone left sharp scissors within reach of a four-year-old boy?" I gasp.

Older eyes roll. It's a miracle anyone survived into adulthood back then with no seat belts and all the expectant mothers smoking Lucky Strikes and sipping martinis. I don't think scissors were on the radar so much.

My dad cut one pant leg off clean at the knee and fashioned some pretty excellent accessories from it. John Wayne would have slapped him right on the back. (Cowboys don't high-five.) But then he was discovered—and was disciplined, of course (likely a stern look over crossed arms)—and he had to promise *never, ever* to do it again. (Now I was the one rolling my eyes.)

My great-grandmother got news of this event and demanded to be in possession of the ruined suit, which was no longer of any use to Grandpa. Nothing was ever wasted. Nothing with any possible use was discarded. This was a generation way ahead of its time. My grandparents were the founding mothers and fathers of Reduce, Reuse, and Recycle. Not to be green but to stay warm, and thus alive.

Dad's grandma actually held onto that suit for twenty-some years. Waiting and waiting. Always inquiring at church or bridge club or the local market about who might have a need for it. At long last, she met a man with one leg and no suit. And to her delight, a little cowboy's mischievous offense hung perfectly on his slight frame.

This is how I picture Paul once Jesus got ahold of him.

Like a one-legged man, partially blind, limping from both exhaustion and injury . . . and relief. In all his travels, perhaps people would see him coming, holding the gospel high, knowing his reputation and the devastation he had brought, and they might stare, slack-jawed at the nerve of this guy. I imagine Paul would acknowledge his guilt quietly and then say something like, "Yeah, but check out my new suit!" A suit that was tailored to accommodate his shortcomings, one he wore with pride because his Lord had been saving it for him. The kind of suit you feel fantastic about wearing when you're going door-to-door with amazingly, unbearably good news.

And so begins his life as an apostle of Christ. A title he would later say he was not worthy to bear, having inflicted so much pain and persecution on the church. At some point, he takes his Roman name, Paul. Maybe because he could more easily take the message of Jesus to the Gentiles without a Jewish name. Or maybe he wanted to disassociate from the historic King Saul, who had ruled with rage and intimidation. Conversely, the origin of the name *Paul* literally means "small," or "humble." Surely he felt at home with those labels now.

We'll never know the real reason he changed his name. Regardless, I love how close it was to the original. It's as if God says we don't need to tear down the whole structure. There was a good man in there somewhere. I remember that man.

I made him. Let's not start over completely; just change the first letter. I've transformed you. I haven't erased you. And you clean up real nice, by the way.

There is so much I can learn from Paul. His adventures, his hardships, his careful concern of those he encouraged and mentored, his love for truth. His fierce commitment to live that truth and not just pay it lip service. He is the original sold-out believer. Urging us into deeper dedication as well.

And he scares me a little.

I have trouble articulating exactly why, but I'll try.

People who have struggled with addiction at some point in their lives will tell you they will always be an addict but, God willing, a recovering one. Alcoholics are always alcoholics, they will say, but some of us just don't drink anymore. We're just one beer away from the rapid descent back into the darkness we created for our lives and for those we love.

I appreciate this definition of recovery. It's so frail. It never asserts victory, never spikes the ball in the end zone. It's a forever kind of path . . . one shaky stone at a time. Slow breathing. Trusting that the guardrail was installed properly along the cliff's edge.

And so I have to wonder, what does a recovering Pharisee look like? Having spent your entire life beating religious law into the collective brow of your audience, strategizing and orchestrating the downfall of anyone who does not play by your rules, wiping their innocent blood on your robe, and thirsting for more control so that you may harvest all the fear you've spent your life nourishing in others. This is how Paul enforced legalism before he met Jesus. Rules. Regulations. Fear. Guidelines. Guilt. Arrogance. Condescension. Self-right-eousness.

How easy was it for Paul, even as a new creature, even as a man wrecked by grace, not to slip back into a leadership role that was marked by suffocating rules and decrees? It must have been tempting. Worn like a second skin. I mean, come on, just one drink? Freedom was a chilling idea for a Pharisee, and also why a grimy, nobody of a janitor hit every panic button possible in him.

I understand that his heart was taken hostage by the blinding light of God's truth. I know he was demolished by his encounter with the Lord's mercy. Believe me, I'm not interested in putting Paul on trial for things Jesus already pardoned him for. (God forbid anyone turn those tables on *me*.) But here's the most scandalous thing I've said since noon: I can still read hints of Pharisee in between the lines of Paul's love letters to his churches. In certain parts, I still smell his need for control. He was still a rules guy. Eat this. Don't eat that. Wear this. Don't wear that. Speak here. Don't speak there. Say this. Not that.

One reason for my discomfort is obvious. I am a woman, and women seemed to be targeted most by all of his regula-tions. And it feels cowardly to sidestep my own questions for Paul. Please don't send me hate mail.

To say that he didn't have a high view of women is an understatement. He also shared some rather poignant thoughts about slavery, but they are easily swept under the rug of cultural context. So why am I still fretting about Paul's teaching on women? I would so much rather study what Jesus had to say about women, honoring us, forgiving us, loving us, getting us. I read some of Paul's teaching, and I start chewing my cuticles into a nervous, bloody mess. I hear the words of Jesus and know I'm okay. My nails will grow back.

A lot of Christian women struggle with this, even if they won't admit it in the town square. It's confusing. Which of Paul's litany of rules do we worry about, and which do we shrug off? I, for one, have really thin and wimpy hair that looks absurd when I braid it, so I'm good on the braid rule.

I will even go as far as saying that I suspect there was good reasoning behind Paul's rules. They were likely well intentioned and appropriate at the time. Maybe he was addressing groups of people who were struggling specifically with certain issues and needed boundaries that perhaps others did not. When you are obsessed with your wealth, and you show up on Sunday morning having sewn gold coins into your hair to display for all, I think it's more than appropriate for someone to say, "Uh, no. No more braids for you. No more gold either." In context, more of what he says must make sense. But most women I know are exhausted by his teaching on this kind of thing, so we just ignore it.

Maybe worse than ignoring it is dismissing it all together. Throwing every last baby out with all that legalistic bathwater.

I think in the end it comes down to a personality issue. Paul is so in your face about everything. For someone like me, who avoids conflict and confrontation at all costs, his delivery is so jarring. So "my way or the highway."

I steer clear of these people in real life. I've been guilty of steering very clear of Paul for the same reason. But really, it was this same "take no prisoners" approach that jettisoned the love of a Jewish messiah into the hearts of the reluctant Gentiles. Who else could have done it? Not me. I'd be handing out brochures entitled, "Hey, check out Jesus, if it's not too much trouble."

Paul might battle fiercely with legalism at times, but he is evermore fierce about grace.

I think he was running with his whole heart, full speed ahead after God's dreams for his people. I think he would stop at nothing to make right what he had once made so wrong.

He knew that Jesus came to abolish the law. Paul himself uses the word *grace* twenty-four times in the book of Romans alone. He understood that it was a gift to be given without expectation or return. But he was a just man. A sinner. A recovering Pharisee. His demons were capable of resurfacing, like anyone's demons. Like the alcoholic whose mouth goes dry at the sight of condensation on a chilled glass of champagne.

Maybe Paul struggled for a lifetime to distance himself from his pharisaical tendencies. Is this any different from my lifelong struggle to abandon apathy? Are we not both in love with the same grace that covers us completely? Is it so far-fetched to think that some of what has spilled onto the pages of the New Testament are the ideals of a man who got caught occasionally between the servant leader he longed to be and the elitist he once was?

Are we not all trapped between old and new at times?

I think if I can continue to look at Paul compassionately, and not defensively, I will stop skipping over certain sections of his writing. If I can find the Pharisee's face in my own mirror and remember how much easier it is to point and judge and create criteria for people: rules and regulations that trump love. Hoops and hoops of principles that acceptance must first jump through. If I can remember how exhausting my own complicated version of religion can be, how much it wears God out, then maybe I won't be exhausted by anyone else's. And we can finally move on to more important topics, like grace. What Jesus is really trying to accomplish outskirts the arguments.

And then Paul and I can finally head out for that cup of coffee.

I'm buying, I tell him.

You can't buy. You're a girl, he says.

(*Sigh.*) Fine. Cream or sugar?

A little of each, thanks.

Hey, I like your suit.

Isn't it perfect? Some kid tried to turn it into a cowboy vest, which is kinda fitting, don't you think?

(*Laughing.*) I do. You are a bit of a trailblazer.

How's your coffee?

It's fine, I lie at first. Actually, it's not fine. It's a little lukewarm.

No problem, he says. I'm just gonna go heat it up.

*But because God was so gracious, so very generous, here I am.*
*And I'm not about to let his grace go to waste.*
*(1 Corinthians 15:10 MSG)*

## move in me
### *paul*
Lyrics from *Music Inspired by The Story*

The man I buried had a heart of stone,
Left him there in the bright light out on a dirt road
The day you saved me from shadow and shame,
Old things gone, got a new song, got a new name.

Burnin' like a wildfire, kickin' up flames,
A brand-new man in a wasteland singing about grace.
Gonna jump the fences until the world is free
But I won't make a move until you move in me.

I'm knocking on doors,
You're keeping the keys.
Maybe they'll open, maybe they're not for me.

I'm setting the sails, you ready the seas,
But I won't make a move until you move in me.

Gonna sing a little louder, gonna rattle these chains.
Locked up tight round midnight, won't stay that way.
Gonna bless this dirt floor, gonna kiss these walls,
Singing your praise until the earth shakes
And watching them fall.

_the second coming_
# the end of the beginning

CHARLIE ATTENDED KINDERGARTEN at a small Christian school where everybody pretty much knew everyone else. A tight-knit bunch. A safe-and-loving launching pad for my little guy to hurl high into the heavens of academia for the first time.

It did not go well at first.

We sat together on a bench outside his classroom each morning for the first five weeks while he sobbed and sobbed and tried to crawl into my purse, hoping it might lead back to my uterus. Finally, his teacher would lovingly scoop him up with hugs and whispers and transplant him onto the circle-time mat while I convulsed my way back through the parking lot and called my mom in hysterics. This went on for twenty-five consecutive school days. So, so, so hard to let go.

(Years later, I found it odd that when I dropped off Pepper at preschool for the first time, I nearly broke my wrist cartwheeling through the parking lot back to my car. Apparently, I was ready for a few hours alone. As was she.)

A week before kindergarten graduation, I got an e-mail from Charlie's teacher. One of his classmates had lost her grandfather due to a heart attack over the weekend. Even worse, she was essentially being raised by her grandparents, and this was the only daddy this sweet girl had ever known. The teacher was encouraging all of the parents to carefully explain to our kids why Libby needed some extra kindness and why she might be having a tough time.

I sat Charlie down and said something carefully like, "Buddy, I know this is a little tough, and I'll try to answer any questions you have, but Libby's grandpa died the other day. She is incredibly sad, and we need to pray for her. But we also need to be extra sweet to her. Give her lots of room to hurt, but also don't be afraid to give her lots of hugs. It's really hard when someone you love dies."

He stared at me blankly.

"Does that make sense, buddy?"

He continued to stare off into silent space for several minutes, and I started flogging myself, certain he was mentally rehearsing the eventual death of Mommy and Daddy and many other comforting events like tornados and quicksand. I had planted a small seed of fear in his heart that I couldn't take back, and now it would grow into a beanstalk.

Suddenly, he snapped out of it and looked at me directly, scrunching his nose and cocking his head slightly and said, "Soooo. What you're saying is that he's dead."

"Um. Yes, honey, he is. He's dead."

"Aaand he's in heaven with Jesus now? "

"That's right, sweetie. I know it's hard to—"

"WOOOOOOOHHHHHOOOOOOOOOOOOOOO!!!!!!!
YAAAAAAHHHHHH BABYYYYYY!!!!!"

I stared at him, dumbfounded. Pumping two fists in the air and hopping around like he'd just sunk a three-pointer at the buzzer. And then I got it.

We had never really talked about death much, but we'd talked about heaven plenty. In the meadows of his beautiful young mind, he could think of no other response than to celebrate the fact that somebody finally got to actually *be* with Jesus. Like playing catch and everything.

I started laughing and crying at the same time.

It wouldn't be long before the world would begin to inform his views of heaven, and I would be hearing a different tone, one that matched his growing attachment to the stuff of his easy life. "Will I get to take my go-cart? Will there be hamsters? Won't singing all day be kinda boring?"

Finally, I have arrived at a place in my parenting where I feel okay about saying, "I just don't know, sweetheart," and let the sentence be a complete one. I am finding this response does not elicit the kind of free-floating panic I imagined it would in my children. Instead, I think intuitively they deeply value the honesty. And I think (I hope) that same honesty will pave the way for more open questions.

Although he has been thus spared, one day Charlie will likely experience the heartache that comes with losing someone he is extremely close to. And he might be mad and resentful about Jesus cutting in on that dance. Then he'll likely say things like, "It was too soon, " and, "What I wouldn't give for one more hour together." He might swear and rage and sleep a lot and eat nothing. And he will want to crawl out of his skin from all the hurt.

But for that one precious and beautifully untarnished moment, my kindergartner danced and hollered at the very idea that death had ended someone's dreadful separation from Jesus. I'll never forget it.

I think most people will admit that the book of Revelation is no picnic in the park. There are some beautiful "Holy Holy Holy" songs that have been written from its text, but a lot of the imagery is hard to take, with all the horns and beasts and dragons and thrones and emeralds and such. It's like a bad sci-fi comic book. Or maybe a good one, if you like sci-fi. I know people get actual degrees in unearthing all the mysterious end times symbolism, and I don't mean any disrespect to those who really enjoy plunging into that deep end, but I usually swim away for safer and more shallow water.

It freaks me out.

Take this friendly little passage for instance:

> I watched as he opened the sixth seal. There was a
> great earthquake. The sun turned black like sackcloth
> made of goat hair, the whole moon turned blood red,
> and the stars in the sky fell to earth, as figs drop from
> a fig tree when shaken by a strong wind. The heavens

receded like a scroll being rolled up, and every mountain and island was removed from its place.[1]

And even though I understand that we're talking about dreams and metaphor, it makes me want to build a bunker for my family and friends so that when the sun turns black and the moon starts hemorrhaging, we can wait it out with a few Kit Kats and Monopoly. Because I want no part of it.

Instead, I turn my thoughts toward Jesus, descending to earth the same way he went up, as Acts tells us, on a cloud. On a safe, fluffy cloud of kindness, perhaps with a little Vivaldi trumpet number in the background. A literal cloud? A symbolic cloud? I pat my own head with gentle compassion, "I just don't know, sweetheart."

If it all happens in the literal sense of the text, I think that will be scary too. For the grown-ups anyway. All the five-year-olds will probably be hollering and high-fiving each other. I think the rest of us might be hiding behind shrubs, Eden-style. I think there will be another mad dash for fig leaves.

Because I know how it feels to find myself on my knees and on my face before Jesus alone in my room, to hand him my sin and my failure and tell him through small shaky sobs that I can't believe we're here again. And I know how it feels when he hands me Kleenex and rubs my back and calls me Hon. It is agony mixed with deep relief and profound wonder that he would sit cross-legged in my mess. Him. King of all kings. Here. On the floor of all floors.

My deepest worship comes out of those places, but only after my deepest shame.

And that's just me in my room. Alone.

How will it feel when the world, the *whole world* watches him come in those clouds? Will we fall down? Probably. We will duck and cover and hide our faces, but maybe not in worship right away. In panic first, I think. In the soul-crushing understanding that we are seen for who we are. Again. Naked. Ashamed. Sinful. I will probably be looking around frantically for anybody who could vouch for me.

Hey! Remember me? I'm the singer! Wrote that meaningful song I thought you'd like. It's about YOU, Jesus!!! Remember that??

I'll probably also be looking for the really bad guys to drag out of the bushes by their ankles, hoping to create a diversion. I will look left and right and left again. Hiding like a hippo behind a telephone pole. Wishing for an invisibility cloak.

Here's the thing. I have no idea what will actually happen. I struggle with this imagery as much as I struggle to think that Jonah hung out in the acidic stomach of a giant fish for three days before he wiped the barf off and did a big U-turn for God. Everything in me wants to scream METAPHOR!!! Because in the end, my idols have always been logic and reason. I have built many altars to common sense. Laws of gravity. Probability. Likelihood. And a few four-leaf clovers. Also, I struggle with faith that is too second-coming centered. As if we're all just muddling through the foggy bog until he finally shows up. Where is the life in that? Where is the living, breathing love of God in that? Where is thy kingdom come, on earth as it is in heaven? Should not every single day include small crucifixions, sweet resurrections, and quiet second comings of his constant love in our lives?

And yet, just to teach me a lesson, it will probably be an actual cloud. And everyone but me will be snacking on mustard seeds.

But cloud or no cloud, he's coming. I know it. And he will not stop coming for me.

And just as he did in the garden, his gaze will stay fixed on me until I can bear to return it. Maybe he will call out again, "Where are you?" until I can bear to answer from behind the shrub.

And then, when there are no more fig leaves to hide behind, I will fall before him. My knees will bend first from fear and then from the weight of his love. And from the sight of his goodness. From the sight of his here-ness.

The way Moses felt on the mountain.

The way Joseph felt in the well.

The way Daniel felt in the den.

The way his mother felt in a stable.

You came for *me*. You actually came for *me*.

And somewhere, the Creator of the heavens and the earth, both old and new, will whisper again,

*It is good.*

*The Son of Man will come again in his great glory, with all his angels. He will be King and sit on his great throne. (Matthew 25:31 NCV)*

# the great day
## *the second coming*
Lyrics from *Music Inspired by The Story*

We met pain in a garden where we lived a lie.
We met hope in a manger and a baby's cry
Rescued by hands bleeding grace.
Are we ready to see his face?
On the great day.

He will come to claim us with a rushing wind
Blown like fields of wheat, the world will bow
    and bend,
Held between our joy and disbelief.
Every trembling heart will finally face the same way
On the great day.

One day Love will wear the crown,
One day Love will set us free,
Hands up high and faces down,
Angels teaching us to sing
He will be King.
He will be King.

He who scattered us on every distant shore,
He will gather us unto himself once more.
Let the story of our footprints tell
We were walking well, holding high your name
Until the great day.

He will be the new sunrise,
Steal the darkness from our eyes,
When we fail to find the words
Holy, Holy we will cry.

# notes

**Creation. The Beginning of the End**
   1. See Genesis 1:2.
   2. Anne LaMott, *Bird by Bird* (New York: Random House, 1994), 22.

**Adam and Eve. How to Kill a Bird**
   1. Genesis 3:5.

**Abraham and Sarah. What to Expect When You're Not Expecting**
   1. Genesis 15:5 MSG.
   2. Psalm 37:4 NKJV.

**Moses. How to Get Unnoticed**
   1. Nicole Johnson, *The Invisible Woman: A Special Story for Mothers* (Nashville: Thomas Nelson, 2005).
   2. Exodus 17:4 MSG.

**Ruth and Naomi. Bridge and Troubled Water**
   1. Ruth 1:16.

**David. Why We Watch the Bleachers**
   1. Acts 13:22 NKJV.
   2. 2 Samuel 23:5–7 MSG.

**Esther. Gravy Trains**
   1. See 1 Samuel 16:7; Matthew 25:34–40.

**Job. When to Make Soup**
   Walter Brueggemann, *The Prophetic Imagination*, 2nd ed. (Minneapolis: Fortress Press, 2001), 57.

**The Disciples. How to Set a Table**
   1. Gary Chapman, *The 5 Love Languages*, 2nd ed. (Chicago: Northfield Publishing, 1992).
   2. Molly O'Neill, *One Big Table* (New York: Simon & Schuster, 2010).

**Paul. When to Cut Class**
   1. Revelation 3:16 MSG.

**The Second Coming. The End of the Beginning**
   1. Revelation 6:12–14.

# acknowledgments

This book would not exist without Norman Miller at Proper Management. For fifteen years, his friendship and guidance have been among God's greatest generosities in my life.

I'm thankful to Worthy Publishing for their enthusiasm and for the opportunity to publish with them. Thanks to Kris Bearss in particular.

To my editor, Sue Ann Jones, who was so encouraging, I am grateful to her for making the whole editing process actually *(gasp)* enjoyable.

When Al Andrews agreed to share his life-giving words in the foreword, I did the ugly cry. Stumbling into a friendship with Al and Nita has been one of God's more extravagant gestures to me this year. You can find out more about what Al is up to at *www.improbablephilanthropy.com*. One hundred percent of the profits of his beautiful book *The Boy the Kite and the Wind* go to people and programs who need it most.

I am forever indebted to the masterful Bernie Herms, who cowrote the songs with me for *The Story*, and in our conversations about Scripture gave me more to consider than could fit in verse or chorus. Thanks to Randy Frazee for being so gracious and available to answer my questions about the text. Ed Gungor, copastor of Sanctuary Church in Tulsa, has made the Word of God come alive for me again. And that's saying a lot. Specifically, Ed's sermon "When God Does New Things" was a tremendous help to me as I wrote about Creation, as was a beautiful meditation on the topic by Rebecca Braden Nordeman. If you need a church in Tulsa, I'll save you a seat.

I am so thankful to my family and friends who stood on the sidelines, hollering encouragement and handing me tiny paper cups of cold water while I was running by. I'm indebted to my faithful tribe for reading early drafts and praying me toward the finish line, especially Dad, Becky, Mom, and Joe. Their confidence made this race more runnable.

I'd also like to thank the teachers and faculty at Colorado Springs Christian School. For ten years you laid the bedrock of biblical knowledge in my young heart. You could not have prevented my doubting or drifting, but you created a place to return to.

And I need to thank the Lord. (Always a weird thing to type and not just blurt out.) He has been extraordinarily patient and tolerant with my zig-zaggy path of faith. I fear this extraordinary patience might be a terminal requirement on my journey. But despite my ongoing struggle to grasp the role that Scripture is meant to play in our modern lives, I still say the best song lyric ever written is:

Yes, Jesus loves me. The Bible tells me so.

**Nichole Nordeman** is a recording artist and songwriter for Sparrow Records/EMI Christian Music Group, with numerous number-one and Top Ten songs to her credit and cumulative CD sales of over one million. A two-time Gospel Music Association winner for Female Vocalist of the Year, she has won a total of nine Dove Awards, including one recently as the lyricist on the best-selling album, *Music Inspired by The Story*. She lives with her family in Tulsa, OK. This is her first book. Connect with her at *www.nicholenordeman.com* and @nicholenordeman on Twitter.

WORTHY
PUBLISHING

## IF YOU LIKED THIS BOOK . . .

- Tell your friends by going to: www.lovestorybook.org and clicking "LIKE"
- Share the video book trailer by posting it on your Facebook page
- Log on to facebook.com/nicholenordeman page, click "LIKE" and post a comment regarding what you enjoyed about the book
- Tweet "I recommend reading #lovestorybook by @nicholenordeman @Worthypub"
- Hashtag: #lovestorybook
- Subscribe to our newsletter by going to www.worthy publishing.com

WORTHY PUBLISHING
FACEBOOK PAGE

WORTHY PUBLISHING
WEBSITE